Chartered Institut
Management Account

D1352273

This book comes with free EN-gage online resources so that you can s...
This free online resource is not sold separately and is included in the price of the book.

## How to access your on-line resources

You can access additional online resources associated with this CIMA Official book via the EN-gage website at: www.EN-gage.co.uk.

## Existing users

If you are an **existing EN-gage user**, simply log-in to your account, click on the 'add a book' link at the top of your homepage and enter the ISBN of this book and the unique pass key number contained above.

## New users

If you are a new EN-gage user then you first need to register at: www.EN-gage.co.uk. Once registered, Kaplan Publishing will send you an email containing a link to activate your account - please check your junk mail if you do not receive this or contact us using the phone number or email address printed on the back cover of this book. Click on the link to activate your account. To unlock your additional resources, click on the 'add a book' link at the top of your home page. You will then need to enter the ISBN of this book (found on page ii) and the unique pass key number contained in the scratch panel below:

Then click 'finished' or 'add another book'.
Please allow 24 hours from the time you submit your book details for the content to appear in the My Learning and Testing area of your account.

## Your code and information

This code can only be used once for the registration of one book online. This registration will expire when this edition of the book is no longer current - please see the back cover of this book for the expiry date.

## Existing users

If you are an **existing EN-gage user**, simply log-in to your account, click on the 'add a book' link at the top of your homepage and enter the ISBN of this book and the unique pass key number contained above.

# Operational Level

# Paper P1

## Management Accounting

## EXAM PRACTICE KIT

Published by: Kaplan Publishing UK

Unit 2 The Business Centre, Molly Millars Lane, Wokingham, Berkshire RG41 2QZ

**British Library Cataloguing in Publication Data**

A catalogue record for this book is available from the British Library

ISBN: 978-1-78415-317-5

Printed and bound in Great Britain

# CONTENTS

|  | Page |
|---|---|
| Index to questions and answers | iv |
| Examination techniques | v |
| Syllabus guidance, learning objectives and verbs | vii |
| Approach to revision | xi |
| Tables | xix |

## Section

| 1 | Objective Test Questions | 1 |
|---|---|---|
| 2 | Answers to Objective Test Questions | 67 |

Quality and accuracy are of the utmost importance to us so if you spot an error in any of our products, please send an email to mykaplanreporting@kaplan.com with full details.

Our Quality Co-ordinator will work with our technical team to verify the error and take action to ensure it is corrected in future editions.

# INDEX TO QUESTIONS AND ANSWERS

## OBJECTIVE TEST QUESTIONS

| | Page number | |
|---|---|---|
| | Question | Answer |
| Costing techniques (Questions 1 to 38) | 1 | 67 |
| Variance analysis (Questions 39 to 97) | 12 | 77 |
| Decision making (Questions 98 to 135) | 27 | 92 |
| Budgeting (Questions 136 to 193) | 41 | 102 |
| The treatment of uncertainty in decision making (Questions 194 to 220) | 57 | 117 |

# EXAM TECHNIQUES

## COMPUTER-BASED ASSESSMENT

### TEN GOLDEN RULES

1    Make sure you have completed the compulsory 15 minute tutorial before you start exam. This tutorial is available through the CIMA website. You cannot speak to the invigilator once you have started.

2    These exam practice kits give you plenty of exam style questions to practise so make sure you use them to fully prepare.

3    Attempt all questions, there is no negative marking.

4    Double check your answer before you put in the final answer although you can change your response as many times as you like.

5    On multiple choice questions (MCQs), there is only one correct answer.

6    Not all questions will be MCQs – you may have to fill in missing words or figures.

7    Identify the easy questions first and get some points on the board to build up your confidence.

8    Try and allow 15 minutes at the end to check your answers and make any corrections.

9    If you don't know the answer, flag the question and attempt it later. In your final review before the end of the exam try a process of elimination.

10    Work out your answer on the whiteboard provided first if it is easier for you. There is also an onscreen 'scratch pad' on which you can make notes. You are not allowed to take pens, pencils, rulers, pencil cases, phones, paper or notes.

vi

# SYLLABUS GUIDANCE, LEARNING OBJECTIVES AND VERBS

## A AIMS OF THE SYLLABUS

The aims of the syllabus are

- to provide for the Institute, together with the practical experience requirements, an adequate basis for assuring society that those admitted to membership are competent to act as management accountants for entities, whether in manufacturing, commercial or service organisations, in the public or private sectors of the economy;
- to enable the Institute to examine whether prospective members have an adequate knowledge, understanding and mastery of the stated body of knowledge and skills;
- to complement the Institute's practical experience and skills development requirements.

## B STUDY WEIGHTINGS

A percentage weighting is shown against each topic in the syllabus. This is intended as a guide to the proportion of study time each topic requires.

All component learning outcomes will be tested and one question may cover more than one component learning outcome.

The weightings do not specify the number of marks that will be allocated to topics in the examination.

## C LEARNING OUTCOMES

Each topic within the syllabus contains a list of learning outcomes, which should be read in conjunction with the knowledge content for the syllabus. A learning outcome has two main purposes:

1    to define the skill or ability that a well-prepared candidate should be able to exhibit in the examination;

2    to demonstrate the approach likely to be taken by examiners in examination questions.

The learning outcomes are part of a hierarchy of learning objectives. The verbs used at the beginning of each learning outcome relate to a specific learning objective, e.g. Evaluate alternative approaches to budgeting.

The verb 'evaluate' indicates a high-level learning objective. As learning objectives are hierarchical, it is expected that at this level students will have knowledge of different budgeting systems and methodologies and be able to apply them.

A list of the learning objectives and the verbs that appear in the syllabus learning outcomes and examinations follows and these will help you to understand the depth and breadth required for a topic and the skill level the topic relates to.

| Learning objectives | Verbs used | Definition |
|---|---|---|
| **1 Knowledge** | | |
| What you are expected to know | List | Make a list of |
| | State | Express, fully or clearly, the details of/ facts of |
| | Define | Give the exact meaning of |
| **2 Comprehension** | | |
| What you are expected to understand | Describe | Communicate the key features of |
| | Distinguish | Highlight the differences between |
| | Explain | Make clear or intelligible/State the meaning of |
| | Identify | Recognise, establish or select after consideration |
| | Illustrate | Use an example to describe or explain something |
| **3 Application** | | |
| How you are expected to apply your knowledge | Apply | To put to practical use |
| | Calculate/compute | To ascertain or reckon mathematically |
| | Demonstrate | To prove with certainty or to exhibit by practical means |
| | Prepare | To make or get ready for use |
| | Reconcile | To make or prove consistent/ compatible |
| | Solve | Find an answer to |
| | Tabulate | Arrange in a table |
| **4 Analysis** | | |
| How you are expected to analyse the detail of what you have learned | Analyse | Examine in detail the structure of |
| | Categorise | Place into a defined class or division |
| | Compare and contrast | Show the similarities and/or differences between |
| | Construct | To build up or compile |
| | Discuss | To examine in detail by argument |
| | Interpret | To translate into intelligible or familiar terms |
| | Produce | To create or bring into existence |
| **5 Evaluation** | | |
| How you are expected to use your learning to evaluate, make decisions or recommendations | Advise | To counsel, inform or notify |
| | Evaluate | To appraise or assess the value of |
| | Recommend | To advise on a course of action |
| | Advise | To counsel, inform or notify |

# D OBJECTIVE TEST

The most common types of Objective Test questions are:

- multiple choice, where you have to choose the correct answer(s) from a list of possible answers. This could either be numbers or text.
- multiple choice with more choices and answers – for example, choosing two correct answers from a list of eight possible answers. This could either be numbers or text.
- single numeric entry, where you give your numeric answer e.g. profit is $10,000.
- multiple entry, where you give several numeric answers e.g. the charge for electricity is $2000 and the accrual is $200.
- true/false questions, where you state whether a statement is true or false e.g. external auditors report to the directors is FALSE.
- matching pairs of text e.g. the convention 'prudence' would be matched with the statement' inventories revalued at the lower of cost and net realisable value'.
- other types could be matching text with graphs and labelling graphs/diagrams.

In this Exam Practice Kit we have used these types of questions.

Some further guidance from CIMA on number entry questions is as follows:

- For number entry questions, you do not need to include currency symbols or other characters or symbols such as the percentage sign, as these will have been completed for you. You may use the decimal point but must not use any other characters when entering an answer (except numbers) so, for example, $10,500.80 would be input as 10500.80
- When expressing a decimal, for example a probability or correlation coefficient, you should include the leading zero (i.e. you should input 0.5 not .5)
- Negative numbers should be input using the minus sign, for example −1000
- You will receive an error message if you try to enter a character or symbol that is not permitted (for example a '£' or '%' sign)
- A small range of answers will normally be accepted, taking into account sensible rounding

**Guidance re CIMA On-Screen calculator:**

As part of the computer based assessment software, candidates are now provided with a calculator. This calculator is on-screen and is available for the duration of the assessment. The calculator is accessed by clicking the calculator button in the top left hand corner of the screen at any time during the assessment.

All candidates must complete a 15 minute tutorial before the assessment begins and will have the opportunity to familiarise themselves with the calculator and practise using it.

Candidates may practise using the calculator by downloading and installing the practice exam at http://www.vue.com/athena/. The calculator can be accessed from the fourth sample question (of 12).

Please note that the practice exam and tutorial provided by Pearson VUE at http://www.vue.com/athena/ is not specific to CIMA and includes the full range of question types the Pearson VUE software supports, some of which CIMA does not currently use.

The Objective Tests are ninety minute computer-based assessments comprising 60 compulsory questions, with one or more parts. CIMA is continuously developing the question styles within the system and you are advised to try the online website demo at www.cimaglobal.com, to both gain familiarity with assessment software and examine the latest style of questions being used.

x

**PAPER P1** : MANAGEMENT ACCOUNTING

# APPROACH TO REVISION

## Stage 1: Assess areas of strengths and weaknesses

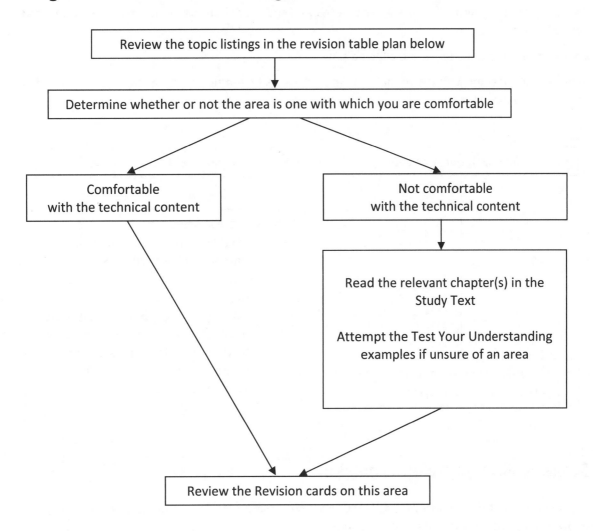

Review the topic listings in the revision table plan below

Determine whether or not the area is one with which you are comfortable

Comfortable
with the technical content

Not comfortable
with the technical content

Read the relevant chapter(s) in the Study Text

Attempt the Test Your Understanding examples if unsure of an area

Review the Revision cards on this area

## Stage 2: Question practice

Follow the order of revision of topics as recommended in the revision table plan below and attempt the questions in the order suggested.

Try to avoid referring to text books and notes and the model answer until you have completed your attempt.

Try to answer the question in the allotted time.

Review your attempt with the model answer and assess how much of the answer you achieved in the allocated exam time.

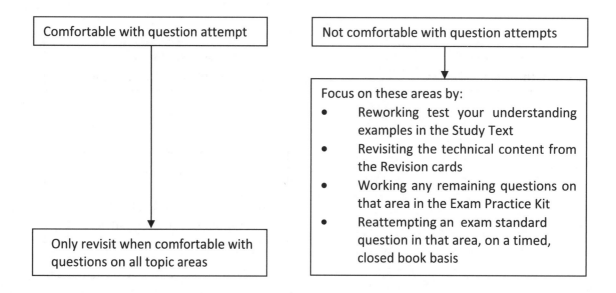

| Comfortable with question attempt | Not comfortable with question attempts |
|---|---|

Focus on these areas by:
- Reworking test your understanding examples in the Study Text
- Revisiting the technical content from the Revision cards
- Working any remaining questions on that area in the Exam Practice Kit
- Reattempting an exam standard question in that area, on a timed, closed book basis

Only revisit when comfortable with questions on all topic areas

## Stage 3: Final pre-exam revision

We recommend that you **attempt at least one ninety minute mock examination** containing a set of previously unseen exam standard questions.

It is important that you get a feel for the breadth of coverage of a real exam without advanced knowledge of the topic areas covered – just as you will expect to see on the real exam day.

Ideally a mock examination offered by your tuition provider should be sat in timed, closed book, real exam conditions.

# P1
# MANAGEMENT ACCOUNTING

## Syllabus overview

P1 stresses the importance of costs and the drivers of costs in the production, analysis and use of information for decision making in organisations. The time focus of P1 is the short term. It covers budgeting as a means of short-term planning to execute the strategy of organisations. In addition it provides competencies on how to analyse information on costs, volumes and prices to take short-term decisions on products and services and to develop an understanding on the impact of risk to these decisions. P1 provides the foundation for cost management and the long-term decisions covered in P2.

## Summary of syllabus

| Weight | Syllabus topic |
|--------|----------------|
| 30% | A. Cost accounting systems |
| 25% | B. Budgeting |
| 30% | C. Short-term decision making |
| 15% | D. Dealing with risk and uncertainty |

## P1 – A. COST ACCOUNTING SYSTEMS (30%)

**Learning outcomes**
On completion of their studies, students should be able to:

| Lead | Component | Indicative syllabus content |
|---|---|---|
| **1 discuss costing methods and their results.** | (a) apply marginal (or variable) throughput and absorption accounting methods in respect of profit reporting and inventory valuation | • Marginal (or variable) throughput and absorption accounting systems of profit reporting and inventory valuation, including the reconciliation of budget and actual profit using absorption and/or marginal costing principles. |
| | (b) compare and contrast activity-based costing with traditional marginal and absorption costing methods | • Product and service costing using an activity-based costing system. <br> • The advantages and disadvantages of activity-based costing compared with traditional costing systems. |
| | (c) apply standard costing methods including the reconciliation of budgeted and actual profit margins, distinguishing between planning and operational variances | • Manufacturing standards for material, labour, variable overhead and fixed overhead. <br> • Standards and variances in service industries, public services (e.g. health and law enforcement), and the professions (e.g. labour mix variances in consultancies). <br> • Price/rate and usage/efficiency variances for materials, labour and variable overhead. <br> • Subdivision of total usage/efficiency variances into mix and yield variances. <br> **Note:** The calculation of mix variances on both individual and average valuation bases is required. <br> • Fixed overhead expenditure and volume variances. <br> • Subdivision of the fixed overhead volume variance into capacity and efficiency variances. <br> • Sales price and sales volume variances (calculation of the latter on a unit basis related to revenue, gross profit and contribution). |

| Learning outcomes<br>On completion of their studies, students should be able to: | | Indicative syllabus content |
|---|---|---|
| **Lead** | **Component** | |
| | | • Sales mix and sales quantity variances.<br>• Application of these variances to all sectors including professional services and retail.<br>• Planning and operational variances.<br>• Variance analysis in an activity-based costing system. |
| | (d) interpret material, labour, variable overhead, fixed overhead and sales variances | • Interpretation of variances.<br>• The interrelationship between variances |
| | (e) explain the advantages and disadvantages of standard costing in various sectors and its appropriateness in the contemporary business environment | • Criticisms of standard costing including its use in the contemporary business environment. |
| | (f) explain the impact of JIT manufacturing methods on cost accounting methods. | • The impact of JIT production on cost accounting and performance measurement systems. |
| **2 discuss the role of quality costing.** | (a) discuss the role of quality costing as part of a total quality management (TQM) system. | • The preparation of cost of quality reports including the classification of quality costs into prevention costs, appraisal costs, internal failure costs and external failure costs.<br>• The use of quality costing as part of a TQM system. |
| **3 explain the role of environmental costing.** | (a) explain the role of environmental costing as part of an environmental management system. | • The classification of environmental costs using the quality costing framework.<br>• Linking environmental costs to activities and outputs and their implication for decision making.<br>• The difficulties in measuring environmental costs and their impact on the external environment.<br>• The contribution of environmental costing to improved environmental and financial performance. |

## P1 – B. BUDGETING (25%)

**Learning outcomes**
On completion of their studies, students should be able to:

| Lead | Component | Indicative syllabus content |
|---|---|---|
| **1 explain the purposes of forecasts, plans and budgets.** | (a) explain the purposes of budgets, including planning, communication, coordination, motivation, authorisation, control and evaluation, and how these may conflict. | • The role of forecasts and plans in resource allocation, performance evaluation and control.<br>• The purposes of budgets, the budgeting process and conflicts that can arise. |
| **2 prepare forecasts of financial results.** | (a) calculate projected product/service volumes, revenue and costs employing appropriate forecasting techniques and taking account of cost structures. | • Time series analysis including moving totals and averages, treatment of seasonality, trend analysis using regression analysis and the application of these techniques in forecasting product and service volumes. |
| **3 discuss budgets based on forecasts.** | (a) prepare a budget for any account in the master budget, based on projections/forecasts and managerial targets. | • The budget setting process, limiting factors, the interaction between component budgets and the master budget. |
|  | (b) discuss alternative approaches to budgeting. | • Alternative approaches to budget creation, including incremental approaches, zero-based budgeting and activity-based budgets. |
| **4 discuss the principles that underlie the use of budgets for control.** | (a) discuss the concept of the budget as a control system and the use of responsibility accounting and its importance in the construction of functional budgets that support the overall master budget. | • The use of budgets in planning and control e.g. rolling budgets and flexed budgets.<br>• The concepts of feedback and feed-forward control.<br>• Responsibility accounting and the link to controllable and uncontrollable costs. |
| **5 analyse performance using budgets, recognising alternative approaches and sensitivity to variable factors.** | (a) analyse the consequences of 'what if' scenarios. | • 'What if' analysis based on alternate projections of volumes, prices and cost structures.<br>• The evaluation of out-turn performance using variances based on 'fixed' and 'flexed' budgets. |

# P1 – C. SHORT-TERM DECISION MAKING (30%)

**Learning outcomes**
On completion of their studies, students should be able to:

| Lead | | Component | Indicative syllabus content |
|---|---|---|---|
| **1 explain concepts of cost and revenue relevant to pricing and product decisions.** | (a) | explain the principles of decision making, including the identification and use of relevant cash flows and qualitative factors | • Relevant cash flows and their use in short-term decision making.<br>• Consideration of the strategic implications of short-term decisions. |
| | (b) | explain the conflicts between cost accounting for profit reporting and inventory valuation, and information required for decision making | • Relevant costs and revenues in decision making and their relation to accounting concepts. |
| | (c) | explain the issues that arise in pricing decisions and the conflict between 'marginal cost' principles, and the need for full recovery of all costs incurred. | • Marginal and full cost recovery as bases for pricing decisions in the short and long-term. |
| **2 analyse short-term pricing and product decisions.** | (a) | apply relevant cost analysis to various types of short-term decisions | • The application of relevant cost analysis to short-term decisions, including special selling price decisions, make or buy decisions, discontinuation decisions and further processing decisions. |
| | (b) | apply break-even analysis in multiple product contexts | • Multi-product break-even analysis, including break-even and profit/volume charts, contribution/sales ratio, margin of safety etc. |
| | (c) | analyse product mix decisions, including circumstances where linear programming methods are needed to identify 'optimal' solutions | • Simple product mix analysis in situations where there are limitations on product/service demand and one other production constraint.<br>• Linear programming for situations involving multiple constraints.<br>• Solution by graphical methods and simultaneous equations of two variable problems, and the meaning of 'optimal' solutions. |
| | (d) | explain why joint costs must be allocated to final products for financial reporting purposes but why this is unhelpful when decisions concerning process and product viability have to be taken. | • The allocation of joint costs and decisions concerning process and product viability based on relevant costs and revenues. |

## P1 – D. DEALING WITH RISK AND UNCERTAINTY (15%)

**Learning outcomes**
On completion of their studies, students should be able to:

| Lead | Component | Indicative syllabus content |
|------|-----------|------------------------------|
| **1 analyse information to assess risk and its impact on short-term decisions.** | (a) discuss the nature of risk and uncertainty and the attitudes to risk by decision makers | • The nature of risk and uncertainty.<br>• The effect of risk attitudes of individuals on decisions. |
| | (b) analyse risk using sensitivity analysis, expected values, standard deviations and probability tables | • Sensitivity analysis in decision modelling and the use of 'what if' analysis to identify variables that might have significant impacts on project outcomes.<br>• Assignment of probabilities to key variables in decision models.<br>• Analysis of probability distributions of project outcomes.<br>• Standard deviations.<br>• Expected value tables and the value of perfect and imperfect information.<br>• Decision trees for multi-stage decision problems. |
| | (c) apply decision models to deal with uncertainty in decision making. | • Maximin, maximax and minimax regret criteria.<br>• Payoff tables. |

# TABLES

## PRESENT VALUE TABLE

Present value of 1.00 unit of currency, that is $(1+r)^{-n}$ where $r$ = interest rate; $n$ = number of periods until payment or receipt.

| Periods | Interest rates ($r$) | | | | | | | | | |
|---|---|---|---|---|---|---|---|---|---|---|
| ($n$) | 1% | 2% | 3% | 4% | 5% | 6% | 7% | 8% | 9% | 10% |
| 1 | 0.990 | 0.980 | 0.971 | 0.962 | 0.952 | 0.943 | 0.935 | 0.926 | 0.917 | 0.909 |
| 2 | 0.980 | 0.961 | 0.943 | 0.925 | 0.907 | 0.890 | 0.873 | 0.857 | 0.842 | 0.826 |
| 3 | 0.971 | 0.942 | 0.915 | 0.889 | 0.864 | 0.840 | 0.816 | 0.794 | 0.772 | 0.751 |
| 4 | 0.961 | 0.924 | 0.888 | 0.855 | 0.823 | 0.792 | 0.763 | 0.735 | 0.708 | 0.683 |
| 5 | 0.951 | 0.906 | 0.863 | 0.822 | 0.784 | 0.747 | 0.713 | 0.681 | 0.650 | 0.621 |
| 6 | 0.942 | 0.888 | 0.837 | 0.790 | 0.746 | 0.705 | 0.666 | 0.630 | 0.596 | 0.564 |
| 7 | 0.933 | 0.871 | 0.813 | 0.760 | 0.711 | 0.665 | 0.623 | 0.583 | 0.547 | 0.513 |
| 8 | 0.923 | 0.853 | 0.789 | 0.731 | 0.677 | 0.627 | 0.582 | 0.540 | 0.502 | 0.467 |
| 9 | 0.914 | 0.837 | 0.766 | 0.703 | 0.645 | 0.592 | 0.544 | 0.500 | 0.460 | 0.424 |
| 10 | 0.905 | 0.820 | 0.744 | 0.676 | 0.614 | 0.558 | 0.508 | 0.463 | 0.422 | 0.386 |
| 11 | 0.896 | 0.804 | 0.722 | 0.650 | 0.585 | 0.527 | 0.475 | 0.429 | 0.388 | 0.350 |
| 12 | 0.887 | 0.788 | 0.701 | 0.625 | 0.557 | 0.497 | 0.444 | 0.397 | 0.356 | 0.319 |
| 13 | 0.879 | 0.773 | 0.681 | 0.601 | 0.530 | 0.469 | 0.415 | 0.368 | 0.326 | 0.290 |
| 14 | 0.870 | 0.758 | 0.661 | 0.577 | 0.505 | 0.442 | 0.388 | 0.340 | 0.299 | 0.263 |
| 15 | 0.861 | 0.743 | 0.642 | 0.555 | 0.481 | 0.417 | 0.362 | 0.315 | 0.275 | 0.239 |
| 16 | 0.853 | 0.728 | 0.623 | 0.534 | 0.458 | 0.394 | 0.339 | 0.292 | 0.252 | 0.218 |
| 17 | 0.844 | 0.714 | 0.605 | 0.513 | 0.436 | 0.371 | 0.317 | 0.270 | 0.231 | 0.198 |
| 18 | 0.836 | 0.700 | 0.587 | 0.494 | 0.416 | 0.350 | 0.296 | 0.250 | 0.212 | 0.180 |
| 19 | 0.828 | 0.686 | 0.570 | 0.475 | 0.396 | 0.331 | 0.277 | 0.232 | 0.194 | 0.164 |
| 20 | 0.820 | 0.673 | 0.554 | 0.456 | 0.377 | 0.312 | 0.258 | 0.215 | 0.178 | 0.149 |

| Periods | Interest rates ($r$) | | | | | | | | | |
|---|---|---|---|---|---|---|---|---|---|---|
| ($n$) | 11% | 12% | 13% | 14% | 15% | 16% | 17% | 18% | 19% | 20% |
| 1 | 0.901 | 0.893 | 0.885 | 0.877 | 0.870 | 0.862 | 0.855 | 0.847 | 0.840 | 0.833 |
| 2 | 0.812 | 0.797 | 0.783 | 0.769 | 0.756 | 0.743 | 0.731 | 0.718 | 0.706 | 0.694 |
| 3 | 0.731 | 0.712 | 0.693 | 0.675 | 0.658 | 0.641 | 0.624 | 0.609 | 0.593 | 0.579 |
| 4 | 0.659 | 0.636 | 0.613 | 0.592 | 0.572 | 0.552 | 0.534 | 0.516 | 0.499 | 0.482 |
| 5 | 0.593 | 0.567 | 0.543 | 0.519 | 0.497 | 0.476 | 0.456 | 0.437 | 0.419 | 0.402 |
| 6 | 0.535 | 0.507 | 0.480 | 0.456 | 0.432 | 0.410 | 0.390 | 0.370 | 0.352 | 0.335 |
| 7 | 0.482 | 0.452 | 0.425 | 0.400 | 0.376 | 0.354 | 0.333 | 0.314 | 0.296 | 0.279 |
| 8 | 0.434 | 0.404 | 0.376 | 0.351 | 0.327 | 0.305 | 0.285 | 0.266 | 0.249 | 0.233 |
| 9 | 0.391 | 0.361 | 0.333 | 0.308 | 0.284 | 0.263 | 0.243 | 0.225 | 0.209 | 0.194 |
| 10 | 0.352 | 0.322 | 0.295 | 0.270 | 0.247 | 0.227 | 0.208 | 0.191 | 0.176 | 0.162 |
| 11 | 0.317 | 0.287 | 0.261 | 0.237 | 0.215 | 0.195 | 0.178 | 0.162 | 0.148 | 0.135 |
| 12 | 0.286 | 0.257 | 0.231 | 0.208 | 0.187 | 0.168 | 0.152 | 0.137 | 0.124 | 0.112 |
| 13 | 0.258 | 0.229 | 0.204 | 0.182 | 0.163 | 0.145 | 0.130 | 0.116 | 0.104 | 0.093 |
| 14 | 0.232 | 0.205 | 0.181 | 0.160 | 0.141 | 0.125 | 0.111 | 0.099 | 0.088 | 0.078 |
| 15 | 0.209 | 0.183 | 0.160 | 0.140 | 0.123 | 0.108 | 0.095 | 0.084 | 0.079 | 0.065 |
| 16 | 0.188 | 0.163 | 0.141 | 0.123 | 0.107 | 0.093 | 0.081 | 0.071 | 0.062 | 0.054 |
| 17 | 0.170 | 0.146 | 0.125 | 0.108 | 0.093 | 0.080 | 0.069 | 0.060 | 0.052 | 0.045 |
| 18 | 0.153 | 0.130 | 0.111 | 0.095 | 0.081 | 0.069 | 0.059 | 0.051 | 0.044 | 0.038 |
| 19 | 0.138 | 0.116 | 0.098 | 0.083 | 0.070 | 0.060 | 0.051 | 0.043 | 0.037 | 0.031 |
| 20 | 0.124 | 0.104 | 0.087 | 0.073 | 0.061 | 0.051 | 0.043 | 0.037 | 0.031 | 0.026 |

Please check the CIMA website for the latest version of the maths
tables and formulae sheets in advance of sitting your live assessment.

Cumulative present value of 1.00 unit of currency per annum, Receivable or Payable at the end of each year for $n$ years $\frac{1-(1+r)^{-n}}{r}$

| Periods (n) | Interest rates (r) | | | | | | | | | |
|---|---|---|---|---|---|---|---|---|---|---|
| | 1% | 2% | 3% | 4% | 5% | 6% | 7% | 8% | 9% | 10% |
| 1 | 0.990 | 0.980 | 0.971 | 0.962 | 0.952 | 0.943 | 0.935 | 0.926 | 0.917 | 0.909 |
| 2 | 1.970 | 1.942 | 1.913 | 1.886 | 1.859 | 1.833 | 1.808 | 1.783 | 1.759 | 1.736 |
| 3 | 2.941 | 2.884 | 2.829 | 2.775 | 2.723 | 2.673 | 2.624 | 2.577 | 2.531 | 2.487 |
| 4 | 3.902 | 3.808 | 3.717 | 3.630 | 3.546 | 3.465 | 3.387 | 3.312 | 3.240 | 3.170 |
| 5 | 4.853 | 4.713 | 4.580 | 4.452 | 4.329 | 4.212 | 4.100 | 3.993 | 3.890 | 3.791 |
| 6 | 5.795 | 5.601 | 5.417 | 5.242 | 5.076 | 4.917 | 4.767 | 4.623 | 4.486 | 4.355 |
| 7 | 6.728 | 6.472 | 6.230 | 6.002 | 5.786 | 5.582 | 5.389 | 5.206 | 5.033 | 4.868 |
| 8 | 7.652 | 7.325 | 7.020 | 6.733 | 6.463 | 6.210 | 5.971 | 5.747 | 5.535 | 5.335 |
| 9 | 8.566 | 8.162 | 7.786 | 7.435 | 7.108 | 6.802 | 6.515 | 6.247 | 5.995 | 5.759 |
| 10 | 9.471 | 8.983 | 8.530 | 8.111 | 7.722 | 7.360 | 7.024 | 6.710 | 6.418 | 6.145 |
| 11 | 10.368 | 9.787 | 9.253 | 8.760 | 8.306 | 7.887 | 7.499 | 7.139 | 6.805 | 6.495 |
| 12 | 11.255 | 10.575 | 9.954 | 9.385 | 8.863 | 8.384 | 7.943 | 7.536 | 7.161 | 6.814 |
| 13 | 12.134 | 11.348 | 10.635 | 9.986 | 9.394 | 8.853 | 8.358 | 7.904 | 7.487 | 7.103 |
| 14 | 13.004 | 12.106 | 11.296 | 10.563 | 9.899 | 9.295 | 8.745 | 8.244 | 7.786 | 7.367 |
| 15 | 13.865 | 12.849 | 11.938 | 11.118 | 10.380 | 9.712 | 9.108 | 8.559 | 8.061 | 7.606 |
| 16 | 14.718 | 13.578 | 12.561 | 11.652 | 10.838 | 10.106 | 9.447 | 8.851 | 8.313 | 7.824 |
| 17 | 15.562 | 14.292 | 13.166 | 12.166 | 11.274 | 10.477 | 9.763 | 9.122 | 8.544 | 8.022 |
| 18 | 16.398 | 14.992 | 13.754 | 12.659 | 11.690 | 10.828 | 10.059 | 9.372 | 8.756 | 8.201 |
| 19 | 17.226 | 15.679 | 14.324 | 13.134 | 12.085 | 11.158 | 10.336 | 9.604 | 8.950 | 8.365 |
| 20 | 18.046 | 16.351 | 14.878 | 13.590 | 12.462 | 11.470 | 10.594 | 9.818 | 9.129 | 8.514 |

| Periods (n) | Interest rates (r) | | | | | | | | | |
|---|---|---|---|---|---|---|---|---|---|---|
| | 11% | 12% | 13% | 14% | 15% | 16% | 17% | 18% | 19% | 20% |
| 1 | 0.901 | 0.893 | 0.885 | 0.877 | 0.870 | 0.862 | 0.855 | 0.847 | 0.840 | 0.833 |
| 2 | 1.713 | 1.690 | 1.668 | 1.647 | 1.626 | 1.605 | 1.585 | 1.566 | 1.547 | 1.528 |
| 3 | 2.444 | 2.402 | 2.361 | 2.322 | 2.283 | 2.246 | 2.210 | 2.174 | 2.140 | 2.106 |
| 4 | 3.102 | 3.037 | 2.974 | 2.914 | 2.855 | 2.798 | 2.743 | 2.690 | 2.639 | 2.589 |
| 5 | 3.696 | 3.605 | 3.517 | 3.433 | 3.352 | 3.274 | 3.199 | 3.127 | 3.058 | 2.991 |
| 6 | 4.231 | 4.111 | 3.998 | 3.889 | 3.784 | 3.685 | 3.589 | 3.498 | 3.410 | 3.326 |
| 7 | 4.712 | 4.564 | 4.423 | 4.288 | 4.160 | 4.039 | 3.922 | 3.812 | 3.706 | 3.605 |
| 8 | 5.146 | 4.968 | 4.799 | 4.639 | 4.487 | 4.344 | 4.207 | 4.078 | 3.954 | 3.837 |
| 9 | 5.537 | 5.328 | 5.132 | 4.946 | 4.772 | 4.607 | 4.451 | 4.303 | 4.163 | 4.031 |
| 10 | 5.889 | 5.650 | 5.426 | 5.216 | 5.019 | 4.833 | 4.659 | 4.494 | 4.339 | 4.192 |
| 11 | 6.207 | 5.938 | 5.687 | 5.453 | 5.234 | 5.029 | 4.836 | 4.656 | 4.486 | 4.327 |
| 12 | 6.492 | 6.194 | 5.918 | 5.660 | 5.421 | 5.197 | 4.988 | 4.793 | 4.611 | 4.439 |
| 13 | 6.750 | 6.424 | 6.122 | 5.842 | 5.583 | 5.342 | 5.118 | 4.910 | 4.715 | 4.533 |
| 14 | 6.982 | 6.628 | 6.302 | 6.002 | 5.724 | 5.468 | 5.229 | 5.008 | 4.802 | 4.611 |
| 15 | 7.191 | 6.811 | 6.462 | 6.142 | 5.847 | 5.575 | 5.324 | 5.092 | 4.876 | 4.675 |
| 16 | 7.379 | 6.974 | 6.604 | 6.265 | 5.954 | 5.668 | 5.405 | 5.162 | 4.938 | 4.730 |
| 17 | 7.549 | 7.120 | 6.729 | 6.373 | 6.047 | 5.749 | 5.475 | 5.222 | 4.990 | 4.775 |
| 18 | 7.702 | 7.250 | 6.840 | 6.467 | 6.128 | 5.818 | 5.534 | 5.273 | 5.033 | 4.812 |
| 19 | 7.839 | 7.366 | 6.938 | 6.550 | 6.198 | 5.877 | 5.584 | 5.316 | 5.070 | 4.843 |
| 20 | 7.963 | 7.469 | 7.025 | 6.623 | 6.259 | 5.929 | 5.628 | 5.353 | 5.101 | 4.870 |

## AREA UNDER THE NORMAL CURVE

This table gives the area under the normal curve between the mean and a point $Z$ standard deviations above the mean. The corresponding area for deviations below the mean can be found by symmetry.

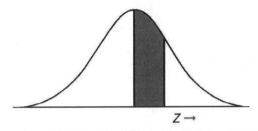

$Z \rightarrow$

| $Z = \dfrac{(x - \mu)}{\sigma}$ | 0.00 | 0.01 | 0.02 | 0.03 | 0.04 | 0.05 | 0.06 | 0.07 | 0.08 | 0.09 |
|---|---|---|---|---|---|---|---|---|---|---|
| 0.0 | .0000 | .0040 | .0080 | .0120 | .0159 | .0199 | .0239 | .0279 | .0319 | .0359 |
| 0.1 | .0398 | .0438 | .0478 | .0517 | .0557 | .0596 | .0636 | .0675 | .0714 | .0753 |
| 0.2 | .0793 | .0832 | .0871 | .0910 | .0948 | .0987 | .1026 | .1064 | .1103 | .1141 |
| 0.3 | .1179 | .1217 | .1255 | .1293 | .1331 | .1368 | .1406 | .1443 | .1480 | .1517 |
| 0.4 | .1554 | .1591 | .1628 | .1664 | .1700 | .1736 | .1772 | .1808 | .1844 | .1879 |
| 0.5 | .1915 | .1950 | .1985 | .2019 | .2054 | .2088 | .2123 | .2157 | .2190 | .2224 |
| 0.6 | .2257 | .2291 | .2324 | .2357 | .2389 | .2422 | .2454 | .2486 | .2518 | .2549 |
| 0.7 | .2580 | .2611 | .2642 | .2673 | .2704 | .2734 | .2764 | .2794 | .2823 | .2852 |
| 0.8 | .2881 | .2910 | .2939 | .2967 | .2995 | .3023 | .3051 | .3078 | .3106 | .3133 |
| 0.9 | .3159 | .3186 | .3212 | .3238 | .3264 | .3289 | .3315 | .3340 | .3365 | .3389 |
| 1.0 | .3413 | .3438 | .3461 | .3485 | .3508 | .3531 | .3554 | .3577 | .3599 | .3621 |
| 1.1 | .3643 | .3665 | .3686 | .3708 | .3729 | .3749 | .3770 | .3790 | .3810 | .3830 |
| 1.2 | .3849 | .3869 | .3888 | .3907 | .3925 | .3944 | .3962 | .3980 | .3997 | .4015 |
| 1.3 | .4032 | .4049 | .4066 | .4082 | .4099 | .4115 | .4131 | .4147 | .4162 | .4177 |
| 1.4 | .4192 | .4207 | .4222 | .4236 | .4251 | .4265 | .4279 | .4292 | .4306 | .4319 |
| 1.5 | .4332 | .4345 | .4357 | .4370 | .4382 | .4394 | .4406 | .4418 | .4430 | .4441 |
| 1.6 | .4452 | .4463 | .4474 | .4485 | .4495 | .4505 | .4515 | .4525 | .4535 | .4545 |
| 1.7 | .4554 | .4564 | .4573 | .4582 | .4591 | .4599 | .4608 | .4616 | .4625 | .4633 |
| 1.8 | .4641 | .4649 | .4656 | .4664 | .4671 | .4678 | .4686 | .4693 | .4699 | .4706 |
| 1.9 | .4713 | .4719 | .4726 | .4732 | .4738 | .4744 | .4750 | .4756 | .4762 | .4767 |
| 2.0 | .4772 | .4778 | .4783 | .4788 | .4793 | .4798 | .4803 | .4808 | .4812 | .4817 |
| 2.1 | .4821 | .4826 | .4830 | .4834 | .4838 | .4842 | .4846 | .4850 | .4854 | .4857 |
| 2.2 | .4861 | .4865 | .4868 | .4871 | .4875 | .4878 | .4881 | .4884 | .4887 | .4890 |
| 2.3 | .4893 | .4896 | .4898 | .4901 | .4904 | .4906 | .4909 | .4911 | .4913 | .4916 |
| 2.4 | .4918 | .4920 | .4922 | .4925 | .4927 | .4929 | .4931 | .4932 | .4934 | .4936 |
| 2.5 | .4938 | .4940 | .4941 | .4943 | .4945 | .4946 | .4948 | .4949 | .4951 | .4952 |
| 2.6 | .4953 | .4955 | .4956 | .4957 | .4959 | .4960 | .4961 | .4962 | .4963 | .4964 |
| 2.7 | .4965 | .4966 | .4967 | .4968 | .4969 | .4970 | .4971 | .4972 | .4973 | .4974 |
| 2.8 | .4974 | .4975 | .4976 | .4977 | .4977 | .4978 | .4979 | .4980 | .4980 | .4981 |
| 2.9 | .4981 | .4982 | .4983 | .4983 | .4984 | .4984 | .4985 | .4985 | .4986 | .4986 |
| 3.0 | .4987 | .4987 | .4987 | .4988 | .4988 | .4989 | .4989 | .4989 | .4990 | .4990 |
| 3.1 | .4990 | .4991 | .4991 | .4991 | .4992 | .4992 | .4992 | .4992 | .4993 | .4993 |
| 3.2 | .4993 | .4993 | .4994 | .4994 | .4994 | .4994 | .4994 | .4995 | .4995 | .4995 |
| 3.3 | .4995 | .4995 | .4995 | .4996 | .4996 | .4996 | .4996 | .4996 | .4996 | .4997 |
| 3.4 | .4997 | .4997 | .4997 | .4997 | .4997 | .4997 | .4997 | .4997 | .4997 | .4998 |

# Section 1

# OBJECTIVE TEST QUESTIONS

All questions in this section carry two marks each, unless otherwise stated.

## COSTING TECHNIQUES

1   A business reported a marginal costing profit of $45,000 last period. Its inventory values for the period were as follows:

|                    | $      |
| ------------------ | ------ |
| Opening inventory  | 16,000 |
| Closing inventory  | 20,800 |

If the business had used absorption costing, the inventory values would have been as follows:

|                    | $      |
| ------------------ | ------ |
| Opening inventory  | 28,000 |
| Closing inventory  | 36,400 |

**What would have been the reported profit using absorption costing?**

A   $41,400

B   $48,600

C   $57,000

D   $60,600

2   A company has a budget to produce 5,000 units of Product B in December. The budget for December shows that, for Product B, the opening inventory will be 400 units and the closing inventory will be 900 units. The monthly budgeted production cost data for Product B for December is as follows:

| | |
| --- | --- |
| Variable direct costs per unit | $6.00 |
| Variable production overhead costs per unit | $3.50 |
| Total fixed production overhead costs | $29,500 |

The company absorbs overheads on the basis of the budgeted number of units produced.

**The budgeted profit for Product B for December, using ABSORPTION COSTING, is:**

A   $2,950 lower than it would be using marginal costing

B   $2,950 greater than it would be using marginal costing

C   $4,700 lower than it would be using marginal costing

D   $4,700 greater than it would be using marginal costing.

**3**     A company operates a standard absorption costing system. The budgeted fixed production overheads for the company for the latest year were $330,000 and budgeted output was 220,000 units.  At the end of the company's financial year the total of the fixed production overheads debited to the Fixed Production Overhead Control Account was $260,000 and the actual output achieved was 200,000 units.

**The under/over absorption of overheads was:**

A     $40,000 over absorbed

B     $40,000 under absorbed

C     $70,000 over absorbed

D     $70,000 under absorbed

**4**     **Company B uses a throughput accounting system.  The details of product X per unit are as follows:**

| | |
|---|---|
| Selling price | €50 |
| Material cost | €16 |
| Conversion costs | €20 |
| Time on bottleneck resource | 8 minutes |

**The return per hour for product X is:**

A     €105

B     €225

C     €255

D     €375

**5**     **A company produces two products, S and T, which pass through two production processes, X and Y.  The time taken to make each product in each process is:**

| | Product S | Product T |
|---|---|---|
| Process X | 5 mins | 7.5 mins |
| Process Y | 18 mins | 12 mins |

The company operates a 15-hour day and have an average downtime each day of:

| | |
|---|---|
| Process X | 1.5 hours |
| Process Y | 1.0 hours |

The costs and revenue for each unit of each product are:

| | Product S | Product T |
|---|---|---|
| | $ | $ |
| Direct materials | 20.00 | 20.00 |
| Direct labour | 18.00 | 14.00 |
| Variable overhead | 4.00 | 4.00 |
| Fixed costs | 5.00 | 4.00 |
| Total cost | 47.00 | 42.00 |
| Selling price | $95.00 | $85.00 |

Sales demand restricts the output of S and T to 50 and 80 units a day respectively.

**Process ___ (enter X or Y) is the bottleneck process.**

6      What is defined as 'an activity within an organisation which has a lower capacity than preceding or subsequent activities, thereby limiting throughput'?

     A      Bottleneck

     B      Constraint

     C      Limiting factor

     D      Restraint

7      A company can produce many types of product but is currently restricted by the number of labour hours available on a particular machine. At present this limitation is set at 12,000 hours per annum. One type of product requires materials costing $5 which are then converted to a final product that sells for $12. Each unit of this product takes 45 minutes to produce on the machine. The conversion costs for the factory are estimated to be $144,000 per annum.

     The throughput accounting ratio for this product is \_\_\_\_\_ *(answer to three decimal places)*.

**The following data relate to Questions 8 and 9.**

The following data relate to a manufacturing company. At the beginning of August there was no inventory. During August 2,000 units of Product X were produced, but only 1,750 units were sold. The financial data for Product X for August were as follows:

|  | $ |
|---|---|
| Materials | 40,000 |
| Labour | 12,600 |
| Variable production overheads | 9,400 |
| Fixed production overheads | 22,500 |
| Variable selling costs | 6,000 |
| Fixed selling costs | 19,300 |
| Total costs for X for August | 109,800 |

8      The value of inventory of X at 31 August using a marginal costing approach is:

     A      $6,575

     B      $7,750

     C      $8,500

     D      $10,562

9      The value of inventory of X at 31 August using a throughput accounting approach is $_____

**10** A manufacturing company recorded the following costs in October for Product X:

|  | $ |
|---|---|
| Direct materials | 20,000 |
| Direct labour | 6,300 |
| Variable production overhead | 4,700 |
| Fixed production overhead | 19,750 |
| Variable selling costs | 4,500 |
| Fixed distribution costs | 16,800 |
| Total costs incurred for Product X | 72,050 |

During October 4,000 units of Product X were produced but only 3,600 units were sold. At the beginning of October there was no inventory.

**The value of the inventory of Product X at the end of October using throughput accounting was:**

A $630

B $1,080

C $1,100

D $2,000

**11** **A business manufactures a single product which sells for $45 per unit. The budgeted data for the latest period are as follows:**

| Production and sales volume | 2,000 units |
|---|---|
|  | $ |
| Material cost | 13,500 |
| Direct labour cost | 11,800 |
| Production overhead | 32,400 |
| Non-production overhead | 21,900 |

Actual production volume and costs were as budgeted for the period but the actual sales volume achieved was 1,800 units. There was no inventory at the beginning of the period.

**The profit for the period using absorption costing is $_____**

**12** **Which of the following statements about JIT is correct?**

A JIT protects an organisation against risks of disruption in the supply chain

B A narrow geographical spread in a business makes JIT more difficult to apply

C With JIT, there is a risk that stocks could become obsolete

D JIT is more difficult to implement when it is not easy to predict patterns of demand

**The following data relate to Questions 13 and 14.**

SM makes two products, Z1 and Z2. Its machines can only work on one product at a time. The two products are worked on in two departments by differing grades of labour. The labour requirements for the two products are as follows:

|  | Minutes per unit of product | |
|---|---|---|
|  | Z1 | Z2 |
| Department 1 | 12 | 16 |
| Department 2 | 20 | 15 |

The current selling prices and costs for the two products are shown below:

|  | Z1 | Z2 |
|---|---|---|
|  | $ per unit | $ per unit |
| Selling price | 50.00 | 65.00 |
| Direct materials | 10.00 | 15.00 |
| Direct labour | 10.40 | 6.20 |
| Variable overheads | 6.40 | 9.20 |
| Fixed overheads | 12.80 | 18.40 |
| Profit per unit | 10.40 | 16.20 |

There is currently a shortage of labour and the maximum times available each day in Departments 1 and 2 are 480 minutes and 840 minutes, respectively.

As part of the budget-setting process, SM needs to know the optimum output levels. All output is sold.

SM has calculated the maximum production of each product as follows and identified Department 1 as the bottleneck in the process:

|  | Z1 | Z2 |
|---|---|---|
|  | Maximum production | Maximum production |
| Department 1 | 480 min/12 min = 40 units | 480 min/16 min = 30 units |
| Department 2 | 840 min/20 min = 42 units | 840 min/15 min = 56 units |

13    Using traditional contribution analysis, calculate the 'profit-maximising' output each day, and the contribution at this level of output.

14    Using a throughput approach, calculate the 'throughput-maximising' output each day, and the 'throughput contribution' at this level of output.

15    Which of the following statements are correct (*tick all that apply)*?

|  |  | Correct? |
|---|---|---|
| (i) | A cost driver is any factor that causes a change in the cost of an activity. |  |
| (ii) | For long-term variable overhead costs, the cost driver will be the volume of activity. |  |
| (iii) | Traditional absorption costing tends to under-allocate overhead costs to low-volume products. |  |

**16** A food-processing company operates an activity based costing (ABC) system. **Determine whether the following would be classified as a facility- or product-sustaining activity** *(place a tick in the box corresponding to any that would apply)*?

|  | | Facility-sustaining | Product-sustaining |
|---|---|---|---|
| (i) | General staff administration | | |
| (ii) | Plant management | | |
| (iii) | Technical support for individual products and services | | |
| (iv) | Updating of product specification database | | |
| (v) | Property management | | |

**17** P operates an activity based costing (ABC) system to attribute its overhead costs to cost objects.

In its budget for the year ending 31 August 20X6, the company expected to place a total of 2,895 purchase orders at a total cost of $110,010. This activity and its related costs were budgeted to occur at a constant rate throughout the budget year, which is divided into 13 four-week periods.

During the four-week period ended 30 June 20X6, a total of 210 purchase orders were placed at a cost of $7,650.

**The over-recovery of these costs for the four-week period was:**

A $330

B $350

C $370

D $390

**18** DRP has recently introduced an Activity Based Costing system. It manufactures three products:

|  | Product D | Product R | Product P |
|---|---|---|---|
| Budgeted annual production (units) | 100,000 | 100,000 | 50,000 |
| Batch size (units) | 100 | 50 | 25 |
| Machine set-ups per batch | 3 | 4 | 6 |
| Purchase orders per batch | 2 | 1 | 1 |
| Processing time per unit (minutes) | 2 | 3 | 3 |
| Budgeted number of batches | 1,000 | 2,000 | 2,000 |

Three cost pools have been identified. Their budgeted costs for 20X4 are as follows:

Machine set-up costs $150,000

Purchasing of materials $70,000

Processing $80,000

**The cost per unit attributed to Product R for machine set ups is $_____**

19    KY makes three products and uses an activity based costing system. The stores receiving costs, which are driven by the number of component deliveries, make up $6,840 of the total production overhead cost.

Driver analysis for KY revealed the following information:

| Product | X | Y | Z |
|---|---|---|---|
| Budgeted production (units) | 1,000 | 1,200 | 800 |
| Number of component deliveries | 500 | 600 | 800 |
| Number of issues from stores | 4,000 | 5,000 | 7,000 |

**The total cost attributed to Product Y for component deliveries using the proposed activity based costing system is $_____**

20    A business manufactures a single product which sells for $45 per unit. The budgeted data for the latest period are as follows:

| | |
|---|---|
| Production and sales volume | 2,000 units |
| | $ |
| Material cost | 13,500 |
| Direct labour cost | 11,800 |
| Production overhead | 32,400 |
| Non-production overhead | 21,900 |

Actual production volume and costs were as budgeted for the period but the actual sales volume achieved was 1,800 units. There was no inventory at the beginning of the period.

**The profit for the period using marginal costing is $_____**

21    T uses a standard labour hour rate to charge its overheads to its clients' work. During the last annual reporting period production overheads were under-absorbed by $19,250. The anticipated standard labour hours for the period were 38,000 hours while the standard hours actually charged to clients were 38,500. The actual production overheads incurred in the period were $481,250.

**The budgeted production overheads for the period were:**

A    $456,000

B    $462,000

C    $475,000

D    $498,000

22    **In the context of quality costs, training costs and reworking costs are classified as:**

| | Training costs | Reworking costs |
|---|---|---|
| A | internal failure costs | external failure costs |
| B | prevention costs | external failure costs |
| C | external failure costs | internal failure costs |
| D | prevention costs | internal failure costs |

**23** WTD Ltd produces a single product. The management currently uses marginal costing but is considering using absorption costing in the future.

The budgeted fixed production overheads for the period are $500,000. The budgeted output for the period is 2,000 units. There were 800 units of opening inventory at the beginning of the period and 500 units of closing inventory at the end of the period.

**If absorption costing principles were applied, the profit for the period compared to the marginal costing profit would be:**

A $75,000 higher

B $75,000 lower

C $125,000 higher

D $125,000 lower

**24 Overheads will always be over-absorbed when:**

A actual output is higher than budgeted output

B actual overheads incurred are higher than the amount absorbed

C actual overheads incurred are lower than the amount absorbed

D budgeted overheads are lower than the overheads absorbed

**25** A business manufactures a single product which sells for $45 per unit. The budgeted data for the latest period are as follows:

| | |
|---|---|
| Production and sales volume | 2,000 units |
| | $ |
| Material cost | 13,500 |
| Direct labour cost | 11,800 |
| Production overhead | 32,400 |
| Non-production overhead | 21,900 |

Actual production volume and costs were as budgeted for the period but the actual sales volume achieved was 1,800 units. There was no inventory at the beginning of the period.

**The profit for the period using throughput accounting is $_____**

**26** S Ltd manufactures three products, A, B and C. The products use a series of different machines but there is a common machine, P, that is a bottleneck.

The selling price and standard cost for each product for the forthcoming year is as follows:

| | A | B | C |
|---|---|---|---|
| | $ | $ | $ |
| Selling price | 200 | 150 | 150 |
| Direct materials | 41 | 20 | 30 |
| Conversion costs | 55 | 40 | 66 |
| | | | |
| Machine P – minutes | 12 | 10 | 7 |

**The return per hour for Product B is $_____**

**27** Match the following examples of costs of quality to the correct classification of quality cost *(draw a line connecting the cost to the classification)*

| Cost |
| --- |
| Staff training |
| Units rejected before delivery |
| Returns of faulty units |
| Finished goods inspection |

| Classification |
| --- |
| Appraisal cost |
| External failure cost |
| Prevention cost |
| Internal failure cost |

**28** Summary results for Y Limited for March are shown below:

|  | $000 | Units |
| --- | --- | --- |
| Sales revenue | 820 | |
| Variable production costs | 300 | |
| Variable selling costs | 105 | |
| Fixed production costs | 180 | |
| Fixed selling costs | 110 | |
| Production in March | | 1,000 |
| Opening inventory | | 0 |
| Closing inventory | | 150 |

Using *marginal costing*, the profit for March was:

A   $170,000

B   $185,750

C   $197,000

D   $229,250

**29** X Ltd has two production departments, Assembly and Finishing, and two service departments, Stores and Maintenance.

Stores provides the following service to the production departments: 60% to Assembly and 40% to Finishing.

Maintenance provides the following service to the production and service departments: 40% to Assembly, 45% to Finishing and 15% to Stores.

The budgeted information for the year is as follows:

Budgeted fixed production overheads

| | |
| --- | --- |
| Assembly | $100,000 |
| Finishing | $150,000 |
| Stores | $50,000 |
| Maintenance | $40,000 |
| Budgeted output | 100,000 units |

At the end of the year after apportioning the service department overheads, the total fixed production overheads debited to the Assembly department's fixed production overhead control account were $180,000.

The actual output achieved was 120,000 units.

**The under-/over-absorption of fixed production overheads for the Assembly department is $_____**

**30** LMN has recently introduced an Activity Based Costing system. It manufactures three products:

|  | Product L | Product M | Product N |
|---|---|---|---|
| Budgeted annual production (units) | 300,000 | 300,000 | 150,000 |
| Batch size (units) | 300 | 150 | 75 |
| Machine set-ups per batch | 4 | 2 | 5 |
| Purchase orders per batch | 2 | 3 | 2 |
| Processing time per unit (minutes) | 4 | 6 | 6 |
| Budgeted number of batches | 5,000 | 4,000 | 4,000 |

Three cost pools have been identified. Their budgeted costs for the year are as follows:

Machine set-up costs $250,000

Purchasing of materials $105,000

Processing $156,000

**The cost per unit attributed to Product L for processing time is $_____**

**31** **A just-in-time (JIT) purchasing system may be defined as:**

A A purchasing system in which the purchase of material is contracted so that the receipts and usage of material coincide

B A purchasing system which is based on estimated demand for finished products

C A purchasing system where the purchase of material is triggered when inventory levels reach a pre-determined re-order level

D A purchasing system which minimises the sum of inventory ordering costs and inventory holding costs

**32** **Which TWO of the following are examples of prevention costs of quality?**

| Cost | Prevention cost? |
|---|---|
| Inspection of raw materials | |
| Routine repairs and maintenance of machinery | |
| Returns of faulty products | |
| Machine breakdown repairs | |
| Training costs of operational staff | |

**33** **Which of the following statements about costs of quality are correct?**

| Cost | True? |
|---|---|
| Conformance costs include prevention costs and appraisal costs | |
| As a company invests in preventing errors, costs of conformance will increase, and costs of non-conformance with fall | |
| Internal failure costs are costs of conformance | |
| External failure costs arise before the product is shipped to the customer | |
| Hiring quality control staff to inspect products is an example of a prevention cost | |

**34** Allberg has incurred the following costs of quality in producing product XY:

| | $ |
|---|---|
| Quality inspector salary | 35,000 |
| Replacing stock damaged in storage | 45,080 |
| Production staff training costs | 5,200 |
| Collection of faulty items from customers | 2,550 |
| Fixing faulty items discovered before delivery | 6,545 |
| | 94,375 |

**What is the total internal failure cost?**

A     $51,625

B     $54,175

C     $86,625

D     $94,375

**35** A company has forecast annual demand of 15,000 units at a selling price of $80 per unit. Contribution is $20 per unit.

However, 17% of items delivered to customers will be returned due to being faulty and require free replacement. The cost of delivering the replacement is $5 per unit.

**What is the cost of external failure?**

A     $76,800

B     $165,750

C     $184,320

D     $199,680

**36** GH produces three models of speedboat for sale to the retail market. GH currently operates a standard absorption costing system. Budgeting information for next year is given below:

| Model of speedboat | Superior | Deluxe | Ultra | Total |
|---|---|---|---|---|
| | $000 | $000 | $000 | $000 |
| Sales | 54,000 | 86,400 | 102,000 | 242,400 |
| Direct material | 17,600 | 27,400 | 40,200 | 85,200 |
| Direct labour | 10,700 | 13,400 | 16,600 | 40,700 |
| Production overhead | | | | 69,600 |
| Gross profit | | | | 46,900 |

| | Superior | Deluxe | Ultra |
|---|---|---|---|
| Production/sales (number of boats) | 1,000 | 1,200 | 800 |
| Machine hours per boat | 100 | 200 | 300 |

The production overhead cost is absorbed using a machine hour rate.

**The total gross profit for the Deluxe speedboat using absorption costing is $_____**

**37**  HZ makes three products and is considering changing to an activity based costing system. The quality inspection costs make up $14,140 of the total production overhead cost.

Driver analysis for HZ revealed the following information:

| Product | A | B | C |
|---|---|---|---|
| Budgeted production | 1,000 | 1,200 | 800 |
| Production units per production run | 5 | 4 | 2 |
| Quality inspections per production run | 10 | 20 | 30 |

**The total cost attributed to Product C for quality inspections using an activity based costing system is $_____**

**38**  **Which of the following explains why an activity based costing system may produce more accurate product costs than a traditional absorption costing system?**

| Cost | Advantage? |
|---|---|
| Better cost control is possible | |
| Arbitrary allocations of costs are avoided | |
| Better product pricing is possible | |
| The choice of cost drivers is easy | |
| Can be applied to service companies | |

# VARIANCE ANALYSIS

**39**  The materials price variance for the month of January was $2,000 (F) and the usage variance was $450 (F). The standard material usage per unit is 6 kg, and the standard material price is $3.00 per kg. 600 units were produced in the period and there was no change in inventory levels during the period.

**Material purchases in the period were:**

A    2,000 kg

B    2,933 kg

C    3,450 kg

D    3,600 kg

**40**  **Which of the following best describes a basic standard?**

A    A standard set at an ideal level, which makes no allowance for normal losses, waste and machine downtime

B    A standard which assumes an efficient level of operation, but which includes allowances for factors such as normal loss, waste and machine downtime

C    A standard which is kept unchanged over a period of time

D    A standard which is based on current price levels

**The following data relate to Questions 41 and 42.**

X40 is one of many items produced by the manufacturing division. Its standard cost is based on estimated production of 10,000 units per month. The standard cost schedule for one unit of X40 shows that 2 hours of direct labour are required at $15 per labour hour. The variable overhead rate is $6 per direct labour hour. During April, 11,000 units were produced; 24,000 direct labour hours were worked and charged; $336,000 was spent on direct labour; and $180,000 was spent on variable overheads.

**41    The direct labour rate variance for April is:**

A    $20,000 Favourable

B    $22,000 Favourable

C    $24,000 Adverse

D    $24,000 Favourable

**42    The variable overhead efficiency variance for April is:**

A    $12,000 Adverse

B    $12,000 Favourable

C    $15,000 Adverse

D    $15,000 Favourable

**The following data relate to Questions 43 and 44.**

X Ltd operates a standard costing system and absorbs fixed overheads on the basis of machine hours. Details of budgeted and actual figures are as follows:

|  | Budget | Actual |
|---|---|---|
| Fixed overheads | $2,500,000 | $2,010,000 |
| Output | 500,000 units | 440,000 units |
| Machine hours | 1,000,000 hours | 900,000 hours |

**43    The fixed overhead expenditure variance is**

A    $190,000 favourable

B    $250,000 adverse

C    $300,000 adverse

D    $490,000 favourable

**44    The fixed overhead volume variance is**

A    $190,000 favourable

B    $250,000 adverse

C    $300,000 adverse

D    $490,000 favourable)

**45**  Y has set the current budget for operating costs for its delivery vehicles, using the formula described below.  Analysis has shown that the relationship between miles driven and total monthly vehicle operating costs is described in the following formula:

$$y = \$800 + \$0.0002x^2$$

where

y is the total monthly operating cost of the vehicles, and

x is the number of miles driven each month

The budget for vehicle operating costs needs to be adjusted for expected inflation in vehicle operating costs of 3%, which is not included in the relationship shown above.

The delivery mileage for September was 4,100 miles, and the total actual vehicle operating costs for September were $5,000.

**The total vehicle operating cost variance for September was closest to:**

A  $713 Adverse

B  $737 Adverse

C  $777 Adverse

D  $838 Adverse

**46**  L uses a standard costing system. The standard cost card for one of its products shows that the product should use 6 kgs of material P per finished unit, and that the standard price per kg is $6.75. L values its inventory of materials at standard prices.

During November 20X1, when the budgeted production level was 2,000 units, 2,192 units were made. The actual quantity of material P used was 13,050 kgs and material L inventories were reduced by 500 kgs. The cost of the material L which was purchased was $72,900.

**The material price and usage variances for November 20X1 were:**

|   | Price | Usage |
|---|-------|-------|
| A | 15,185.50 (F) | 450.00 (F) |
| B | 11,812.50 (F) | 688.50 (F) |
| C | 15,187.50 (F) | 450.00 (A) |
| D | 11,812.50 (F) | 688.50 (A) |

**47**  The CIMA official definition of the 'variable production overhead efficiency variance' is set out below with two blank sections.

'Measures the difference between the variable overhead cost budget flexed on _____ and the variable overhead cost absorbed by _____.'

**Which combination of phrases correctly completes the definition?**

|   | Blank 1 | Blank 2 |
|---|---------|---------|
| A | actual labour hours | budgeted output |
| B | standard labour hours | budgeted output |
| C | actual labour hours | output produced |
| D | standard labour hours | output produced |

**48**   R uses a standard costing system and has the following labour cost standard in relation to one of its products:

10 hours skilled labour at $9.50 per hour = $95.00

**During March 20X9, 6,200 of these products were made which was 250 units less than budgeted.  The labour cost incurred was $596,412 and the number of direct labour hours worked was 62,890. The direct labour variances for the month were:**

|   | Rate | Efficiency |
|---|---|---|
| A | $1,043 (F) | $8,900 (A) |
| B | $7,412 (F) | $8,455 (A) |
| C | $1,043 (F) | $8,455 (A) |
| D | $7,412 (F) | $8,900 (A) |

**49**   P has the following budget and actual data:

| | |
|---|---|
| Budget fixed overhead cost | $170,000 |
| Budget production (units) | 42,500 |
| Actual fixed overhead cost | $182,000 |
| Actual production (units) | 40,000 |

**The adverse fixed overhead volume variance is $_____**

**50**   S has the following budget and actual data:

| | |
|---|---|
| Budget fixed overhead cost | $1,248,480 |
| Budget production (units) | 20,400 |
| Budgeted labour hours | 104,040 |
| Actual fixed overhead cost | $1,366,620 |
| Actual production (units) | 20,000 |
| Actual labour hours | 100,000 |

**The favourable fixed overhead efficiency variance is $_____**

**The following data relate to Questions 51 and 52.**

A hospital uses a standard costing system to monitor the performance of it surgeons. The following information is available for June:

The standard time to perform an eye operation is 2 hours. In June, the budget for eye operations showed that 320 operations would be performed and the (fixed) overheads attributable to eye operations would be $108,000.

The actual results showed that only 300 operations were performed in a total of 660 hours, and that the actual (fixed) overheads were $110,000.

**51**   The fixed overhead capacity variance for June was:

A   $3,375 Adverse

B   $3,375 Favourable

C   $10,125 Favourable

D   $10,125 Adverse

**52** **The fixed overhead efficiency variance for June was:**

A $3,375 Adverse

B $3,375 Favourable

C $10,125 Favourable

D $10,125 Adverse

**The following data relate to Questions 53 and 54.**

Trafalgar budgets to produce 10,000 units of product D12, each requiring 45 minutes of labour. Labour is charged at $20 per hour, and variable overheads at $15 per labour hour. During September, 11,000 units were produced. 8,000 hours of labour were paid at a total cost of $168,000. Variable overheads in September amounted to $132,000.

**53** **What is the labour efficiency variance for September?**

A $5,000 Adverse

B $5,000 Favourable

C $5,250 Favourable

D $10,000 Adverse

**54** **What is the variable overhead expenditure variance for September?**

A $3,750 Favourable

B $,125 Favourable

C $12,000 Adverse

D $12,000 Favourable

**The following data relate to Questions 55 and 56.**

Z sells PCs that it purchases through a regional distributor. An extract from its budget for the 4-week period ended 28 March 20X8 shows that it planned to sell 600 PCs at a unit price of $500, which would give a contribution to sales ratio of 25%.

Actual sales were 642 PCs at an average selling price of $465. The actual contribution to sales ratio averaged 20%.

**55** **The sales price variance (to the nearest $1) was:**

A $22,470 (F)

B $1,470 (A)

C $1,470 (F)

D $22,470 (A)

**56** **The sales volume contribution variance (to the nearest $1) was:**

A $5,050 (F)

B $5,150 (F)

C $5,250 (F)

D $5,350 (F)

**57**   A company has a process in which the standard mix for producing 9 litres of output is as follows:

|  | $ |
|---|---|
| 4.0 litres of D at $9 per litre | 36.00 |
| 3.5 litres of E at $5 per litre | 17.50 |
| 2.5 litres of F at $2 per litre | 5.00 |
|  | 58.50 |

Actual input for this period was 10,000 litres, which included 3,600 litres of E.

**The favourable material mix variance for Product E using the average valuation method was $_____**

**58**   Operation B, in a factory, has a standard time of 15 minutes. The standard rate of pay for operatives is $10 per hour.  The budget for a period was based on carrying out the operation 350 times. It was subsequently realised that the standard time for Operation B included in the budget did not incorporate expected time savings from the use of new machinery from the start of the period. The standard time should have been reduced to 12 minutes.

Operation B was actually carried out 370 times in the period in a total of 80 hours.  The operatives were paid $850.

**The operational labour efficiency variance was:**

A   $60 adverse

B   $75 favourable

C   $100 adverse

D   $125 adverse

**59**   A company input 10,000 litres of liquid into a process which has a standard mix for producing 9 litres of output as follows:

|  | $ |
|---|---|
| 4.0 litres of D at $9 per litre | 36.00 |
| 3.5 litres of E at $5 per litre | 17.50 |
| 2.5 litres of F at $2 per litre | 5.00 |
|  | 58.50 |

A standard loss of 10% of inputs is expected to occur. Actual output for this period was 9,100 litres.

**The materials yield variance was:**

A   $650 adverse

B   $650 favourable

C   $585 adverse

D   $585 favourable

**60    The fixed overhead volume variance is defined as:**

A    the difference between the budgeted value of the fixed overheads and the standard fixed overheads absorbed by actual production

B    the difference between the standard fixed overhead cost specified for the production achieved, and the actual fixed overhead cost incurred

C    the difference between budgeted and actual fixed overhead expenditure

D    the difference between the standard fixed overhead cost specified in the original budget and the same volume of fixed overheads, but at the actual prices incurred

**The following data relate to Questions 61 and 62.**

SW manufactures a product known as the TRD100 by mixing two materials. The standard material cost per unit of the TRD100 is as follows:

|            |           |     |        | $  |
|------------|-----------|-----|--------|----|
| Material X | 12 litres | @   | $2.50  | 30 |
| Material Y | 18 litres | @   | $3.00  | 54 |

In October 20X3, the actual mix used was 984 litres of X and 1,230 litres of Y. The actual output was 72 units of TRD100.

**61    The total favourable material mix variance for October 20X3 was $_____ (round to 1 decimal place).**

**62    The total adverse material yield variance for October 20X3 was $_____ (round to 1 decimal place).**

**63    Which of the following events would help to explain an adverse material usage variance (place a tick for all those that apply)?**

|       |                                                                                             | Correct? |
|-------|---------------------------------------------------------------------------------------------|----------|
| (i)   | The standard allowance for material wastage was set too high.                               |          |
| (ii)  | Material purchased was of a lower quality than standard.                                    |          |
| (iii) | Lower grade and less experienced employees were used than standard.                        |          |
| (iv)  | More material was purchased than budgeted for the period because output was higher than budgeted. |          |

**64    A company operates a standard absorption costing system. The following fixed production overhead data are available for the latest period:**

| Budgeted output | 300,000 units |
|---|---|
| Budgeted fixed production overhead | $1,500,000 |
| Actual fixed production overhead | $1,950,000 |
| Fixed production overhead total variance | $150,000 adverse |

**The actual level of production for the period was _____ units (round to the nearest 1,000 units)**

**65**    Which of the following is the most likely to result in an adverse variable overhead efficiency variance?

   A     Higher bonus payments to employees than standard

   B     Less experienced employees were used than standard

   C     The use of more expensive, higher quality materials than standard

   D     Machine power costs per hour were higher than standard

---

**The following data relate to Questions 66 and 67.**

A cleaning material, X2, is manufactured by mixing three materials. Standard cost details of the product are as follows.

**Cost per batch of 10 litres of X2**

|            |          |   |      | $   |
|------------|----------|---|------|-----|
| Material C | 6 litres | @ | $3   | 18  |
| Material D | 3 litres | @ | $1   | 3   |
| Material E | 1 litre  | @ | $5   | 5   |
|            | 10       |   |      | 26  |

In the latest period, the actual mix used was 200 litres of C, 75 litres of D and 25 litres of E. The output achieved was 280 litres of cleaning material X2.

---

**66**    Using the average valuation basis, the adverse material mix variance for Material C was $_____

**67**    The total adverse material yield variance was $_____

**68**    PQR Ltd operates a standard absorption costing system. Details of budgeted and actual figures are as follows:

|                          | Budget   | Actual   |
|--------------------------|----------|----------|
| Sales volume (units)     | 100,000  | 110,000  |
| Selling price per unit   | $10      | $9.50    |
| Variable cost per unit   | $5       | $5.25    |
| Total cost per unit      | $8       | $8.30    |

The favourable sales volume profit variance for the period was $_____

**69**    During a period, the staff of A worked 200 hours more than had been planned in the original budget, and 100 hours more than the standard time to produce the actual output. This would have caused which of the following variances.

   A     Favourable labour efficiency variance

   B     Adverse fixed overhead volume variance

   C     Favourable fixed overhead efficiency variance

   D     Favourable fixed overhead capacity variance

---

**70** A company manufactures a fruit flavoured drink concentrate by mixing two liquids (X and Y). The standard cost card for ten litres of the drink concentrate is:

|  |  |  | $ |
|---|---|---|---|
| Liquid X | 5 litres | @ $16 per litre | 80 |
| Liquid Y | 6 litres | @ $25 per litre | 150 |
|  | 11 litres |  | 230 |

The company does not hold any inventory. During the last period the company produced 4,800 litres of the drink concentrate. This was 200 litres below the budgeted output. The company purchased 2,200 litres of X for $18 per litre and 2,750 litres of Y for $21 per litre.

**The materials mix variance for the period was:**

A $150 adverse

B $450 adverse

C $6,480 favourable

D $6,900 favourable

---

**The following data relate to Questions 71 and 72.**

A company has a process in which three inputs are mixed together to produce Product S. The standard mix of inputs to produce 90 kg of Product S is shown below:

|  | $ |
|---|---|
| 50 kg of ingredient P at $75 per kg | 3,750 |
| 30 kg of ingredient Q at $100 per kg | 3,000 |
| 20 kg of ingredient R at $125 per kg | 2,500 |
|  | 9,250 |

During March 2,000 kg of ingredients were used to produce 1,910 kg of Product S. Details of the inputs are as follows:

|  | $ |
|---|---|
| 1,030 kg of ingredient P at $70 per kg | 72,100 |
| 560 kg of ingredient Q at $106 per kg | 59,360 |
| 410 kg of ingredient R at $135 per kg | 55,350 |
|  | 186,810 |

---

**71** **The materials mix variance for March was:**

A $110 adverse

B $500 adverse

C $110 favourable

D $500 favourable

---

72    **Calculate the materials yield variance for March was:**

A    $11,306 adverse

B    $500 adverse

C    $11,306 favourable

D    $500 favourable

**The following data relate to Questions 73 to 75.**

The following data relate to Product Z and its raw material content for September:

*Budget*

| | |
|---|---|
| Output | 11,000 units of Z |
| Standard materials content | 3 kg per unit at $4.00 per kg |

*Actual*

| | |
|---|---|
| Output | 10,000 units of Z |
| Materials purchased and used | 32,000 kg at $4.80 per kg |

It has now been agreed that the standard price for the raw material purchased in September should have been $5 per kg.

73    **Using actual units produced, the materials planning price variance for September was:**

A    $6,000 Adverse

B    $30,000 Adverse

C    $32,000 Adverse

D    $33,000 Adverse

74    **The materials operational usage variance for September was:**

A    $8,000 Adverse

B    $9,600 Adverse

C    $9,600 Favourable

D    $10,000 Adverse

75    **The materials operational price variance for September was:**

A    $6,000 Adverse

B    $6,400 Favourable

C    $30,000 Adverse

D    $32,000 Adverse

**The following data relate to Questions 76 and 77.**

Q plc uses standard costing. The details for April were as follows:

| | | |
|---|---|---|
| Budgeted output | 15,000 | units |
| Budgeted labour hours | 60,000 | hours |
| Budgeted labour cost | $540,000 | |
| | | |
| Actual output | 14,650 | units |
| Actual labour hours paid | 61,500 | hours |
| Productive labour hours | 56,000 | hours |
| Actual labour cost | $522,750 | |

**76     The idle time variance for April was $_____**

**77     The favourable labour efficiency variance for April was $_____**

**The following data relate to Questions 78 to 80.**

A company uses standard absorption costing. The following information was recorded by the company for October:

| | Budget | Actual |
|---|---|---|
| Output and sales (units) | 8,700 | 8,200 |
| Selling price per unit | $26 | $31 |
| Variable cost per unit | $10 | $10 |
| Total fixed overheads | $34,800 | $37,000 |

**78     The sales price variance for October was:**

   A     $38,500 Favourable

   B     $41,000 Favourable

   C     $41,000 Adverse

   D     $65,600 Adverse

**79     The sales volume profit variance for October was:**

   A     $6,000 Adverse

   B      $6,000 Favourable

   C     $8,000 Adverse

   D     $8,000 Favourable

**80     The fixed overhead volume variance for October was:**

   A     $2,000 Adverse

   B     $2,200 Adverse

   C     $2,200 Favourable

   D     $4,200 Adverse

**The following data relate to Questions 81 and 82.**

PP Ltd operates a standard absorption costing system. The following information has been extracted from the standard cost card for one of its products:

| | |
|---|---|
| Budgeted production | 1,500 units |
| Direct material cost: 7 kg × $4.10 | $28.70 per unit |

Actual results for the period were as follows:

| | |
|---|---|
| Production | 1,600 units |
| Direct material (purchased and used): 12,000 kg | $52,200 |

It has subsequently been noted that, owing to a change in economic conditions, the best price that the material could have been purchased for was $4.50 per kg during the period.

**81** **The adverse material price planning variance was $_____**

**82** **The adverse operational material usage variance was $_____**

**83** SS Ltd operates a standard marginal costing system. An extract from the standard cost card for the labour costs of one of its products is as follows:

Labour cost
5 hours × $12                 $60

Actual results for the period were as follows:

| | |
|---|---|
| Production | 11,500 units |
| Labour rate variance | $45,000 adverse |
| Labour efficiency variance | $30,000 adverse |

**The actual rate paid per direct labour hour for the period was $_____**

**84** During a period, Jones had the following budgeted and actual sales:

| | Product A | Product B |
|---|---|---|
| Sales budget (units) | 800 | 800 |
| Actual sales (units) | 750 | 700 |
| Standard profit per unit | $5.00 | $3.00 |

**The total favourable sales mix profit variance for the period using the individual units method is $_____**

**85** **Match the variance with its most likely cause (draw a line connecting the variance to the correct cause)**

| Variance | | Cause |
|---|---|---|
| Material price variance | | Increased wastage due to a machine malfunction |
| Material usage variance | | Unexpected pay award |
| Labour rate variance | | Increase in costs charged by a supplier |
| Labour efficiency variance | | Improved operating procedures for staff. |

**86**   During a period, Jones had the following budgeted and actual sales:

|                          | Product A | Product B |
|--------------------------|-----------|-----------|
| Sales budget (units)     | 800       | 800       |
| Actual sales (units)     | 750       | 700       |
| Standard profit per unit | $5.00     | $3.00     |

The total adverse sales quantity profit variance for the period is $_____

**87**   During a period, A Ltd had the following budgeted and actual sales:

|                         | Product A | Product B | Product C |
|-------------------------|-----------|-----------|-----------|
| Sales budget (units)    | 3,000     | 8,000     | 9,000     |
| Actual sales (units)    | 4,000     | 7,500     | 11,500    |
| Standard price per unit | $10.00    | $8.00     | $5.00     |
| Actual price per unit   | $9.50     | $8.75     | $4.00     |
| Budgeted cost per unit  | $8.00     | $6.50     | $3.20     |
| Actual cost per unit    | $8.00     | $6.50     | $3.20     |

The total favourable sales mix profit variance for the period using the individual units method is $_____

**88**   During a period, A Ltd had the following budgeted and actual sales:

|                         | Product A | Product B | Product C |
|-------------------------|-----------|-----------|-----------|
| Sales budget (units)    | 3,000     | 8,000     | 9,000     |
| Actual sales (units)    | 4,000     | 7,500     | 11,500    |
| Standard price per unit | $10.00    | $8.00     | $5.00     |
| Actual price per unit   | $9.50     | $8.75     | $4.00     |
| Budgeted cost per unit  | $8.00     | $6.50     | $3.20     |
| Actual cost per unit    | $8.00     | $6.50     | $3.20     |

The total favourable sales quantity profit variance for the period is $_____

**89**   Which two of the following variances are most likely to be directly caused by purchasing better quality materials?

|                                                  | Caused by purchasing better quality? |
|--------------------------------------------------|--------------------------------------|
| Favourable fixed overhead expenditure variance   |                                      |
| Favourable material usage variance               |                                      |
| Adverse labour rate variance                     |                                      |
| Favourable labour efficiency variance            |                                      |
| Favourable labour rate variance                  |                                      |

**90**   Which of the following managers is most likely to be responsible for an adverse labour efficiency variance?

A   Production manager

B   Purchasing manager

C   Human resources manager

D   Finance manager

**91** PQ produces two products, Product B and Product C. The following budget and actual data relate to August:

|  | Product B | Product C |
|---|---|---|
| **Budget data:** | | |
| Production and sales | 2,200 units | 1,800 units |
| Standard contribution per unit | $58.00 | $59.75 |
| Standard profit per unit | $50.00 | $53.75 |
| **Actual data:** | | |
| Production and sales | 3,000 units | 1,500 units |

The favourable sales mix variance for Product B is $_____ (*use the individual units method*)

**92** Which of the following managers is most likely to be responsible for an adverse materials price variance?

A Production manager

B Purchasing manager

C Human resources manager

D Finance manager

**93** Annabelle uses activity based costing to allocate its overheads. There some differences between the actuals and the standard and the production manager is confused. The standard cost expected for the Setups cost pool were:

| Budgeted units | 22,000 |
|---|---|
| Budgeted setups | 220 |
| Budgeted cost | $6,820 |

The Actual costs incurred were

| Actual units | 21,000 |
|---|---|
| Actual setups | 200 |
| Actual cost | $6,300 |

The expenditure variance for the setups was $_____

**94** Which of the following variances would be affected if the company switched from an absorption costing system to a marginal costing system?

|  | Affected? |
|---|---|
| Sales price variance | |
| Sales quantity profit variance | |
| Direct labour rate variance | |
| Fixed overhead expenditure variance | |
| Fixed overhead capacity variance | |

**95** Alderholt uses activity based costing to allocate its overheads. The following information is provided for the supervisor cost:

|  | Budget | Actual |
|---|---|---|
| Total employees | 5,000 | 5,500 |
| Number of supervisors | 75 | 77 |
| Supervisor cost | $7,500 | $8,085 |

**What was the total variance for the supervisor cost?**

A    $585 Adverse

B    $165 Favourable

C    $5550 Favourable

D    $385 Adverse

**96** A company produces two products with the following standard information:

|  | Product X | Product Y |
|---|---|---|
| *Production and sales* | *10,000 units* | *18,000 units* |
| Direct labour ($7 per hour) | $14.00 | $10.50 |
| Variable overhead | $3.00 | $2.25 |

The company actually spent $87,140 on variable overheads, whilst labour worked for 46,000 hours. 12,000 units of X and 16,000 units of Y were produced.

**The adverse variable overhead efficiency variance is $_____**

**97** FF produces two products, Product R and Product S. The following budget and actual data was prepared for the period:

|  | Product R | Product S |
|---|---|---|
| **Budget data:** |  |  |
| Production and sales | 4,000 units | 6,000 units |
| Standard contribution per unit | $6 | $8 |
| Standard profit per unit | $4 | $3 |
| **Actual data:** |  |  |
| Production and sales | 6,000 units | 6,000 units |

**The sales quantity profit variance for Product S using the weighted average method is:**

A    $0

B    $2,720

C    $4,080

D    $6,800

# DECISION MAKING

**98** An organisation is considering the costs to be incurred in respect of a special order opportunity.

The order would require 1,250 kgs of material D. This is a material that is readily available and regularly used by the organisation on its normal products. There are 265 kgs of material D in stock which cost $795 last week. The current market price is $3.24 per kg.

Material D is normally used to make product X. Each unit of X requires 3 kgs of material D, and if material D is costed at $3 per kg, each unit of X yields a contribution of $15.

**The relevant cost of material D to be included in the costing of the special order is nearest to:**

A    $3,990

B    $4,050

C    $10,000

D    $10,300

**99** A company has budgeted breakeven sales revenue of $800,000 and fixed costs of $320,000 for the next period.

**The sales revenue needed to achieve a profit of $50,000 in the period would be:**

A    $850,000

B    $925,000

C    $1,120,000

D    $1,200,000

**100** H Ltd has in stock 15,000 kg of M, a raw material which it bought for $3/kg five years ago, for a product line which was discontinued four years ago.

At present, M has no use in its existing state but could be sold as scrap for $1.00 per kg. One of the company's current products (HN) requires 4 kg of a raw material which is available for $5.00 per kg.  M can be modified at a cost of $0.75 per kg so that it may be used as a substitute for this material.  However, after modification, 5 kg of M is required for every unit of HN to be produced.

H Ltd has now received an invitation to tender for a product which could use M in its present state.

**The relevant cost per kg of M to be included in the cost estimate for the tender is:**

A    $0.75

B    $1.00

C    $3.00

D    $3.25

**101** UU Company has been asked to quote for a special contract which will require material X. The following information is available on material X:

| Book value | Scrap value | Replacement cost |
|---|---|---|
| $5.00 per kg | $0.50 per kg | $5.50 per kg |

The special contract would require 10 kgs of Material X. There are 250 kgs of this material in stock which was purchased in error over two years ago. It has just been noticed that if Material X is modified, at a cost of $2 per kg, it could then be used as a substitute for material Y which is in regular use and currently costs $6 per kg.

**The relevant cost of the materials for the special contract is:**

A $5

B $40

C $50

D $55

**102** A company has been asked to quote for a special contract. The following information is available on the labour required for the contract:

The special contract would require 100 hours of labour. However, the labourers, who are each paid $15 per hour, are working at full capacity. There is a shortage of labour in the market and therefore the labour required to undertake this special contract would have to be taken from another contract, Z, which currently utilises 500 hours of labour and generates $5,000 worth of contribution. If the labour was taken from contract Z, then the whole of contract Z would have to be delayed, and such delay would invoke a penalty fee of $1,000.

A $1,000

B $1,500

C $2,500

D $7,500

**103** A company is preparing a quotation for a one-month consultancy project. Currently the company employs a consultant on an annual salary of $36,000.

This consultant is fully employed on current projects and, if she were to be transferred to this new project, then an existing junior consultant would be used to cover her current work. The junior consultant would be paid a bonus of $5,000 for undertaking this additional responsibility.

Alternatively the company could hire an external consultant on a one month contract at a cost of $4,500.

**The relevant cost to be used in preparing the quotation is:**

A $4,500

B $5,000

C $40,500

D $41,000

**104** Jones Company is bidding for a contract which is due to be started within a few days. The contract will use up its stock of Material XY which will otherwise be held for one month. In one month's time, there is a probability of 0.6 that it will be used. If it is not used then the material will be sold. Estimates are as follows:

|  | $ |
|---|---|
| Replacement cost of stock in one month's time | 15,000 |
| Sales value in one month's time | 12,000 |
| Stock holding cost for one month | 900 |

**The expected relevant cost of Material XY for use when evaluating the viability of the contract is $_____**

**105** A company is calculating the relevant cost of the material to be used on a particular contract.

The contract requires 4,200 kgs of material H and this can be bought for $6.30 per kg.

The company bought 10,000 kgs of material H some time ago when it paid $4.50 per kg. Currently 3,700 kgs of this remains in stock. The stock of material H could be sold for $3.20 per kg.

The company has no other use for material H other than on this contract, but it could modify it at a cost of $3.70 per kg and use it as a substitute for material J. Material J is regularly used by the company and can be bought for $7.50 per kg.

**The relevant cost of the material for the contract is:**

A       $17,210

B       $19,800

C       $26,460

D       $30,900

**106** A company manufactures two joint products and a by-product in a single process, which are all sold as soon as they are output from the process, without further processing. Joint costs are shared on the basis of sales value at the split-off point and the revenue from the by-product is credited to the cost of production.

The budget for the next period is as follows:

Processing costs: $45,000

Output in units:

Joint product X – 250 units

Joint product Y – 400 units

By-product Z – 3,000 units

Selling prices per unit: $80 for X, $100 for Y, $0.20 for Z.

**The cost per unit of product Y is $_____**

**107** FPG Company sells three products – F, P and G. The ratio of their total sales values is 6F : 5P : 4G. The contribution to sales ratios of the products are:

F 35%          P 20%          G 30%

**If fixed costs for the period are expected to be $160,000, the revenue (to the nearest $1,000) needed to earn a marginal costing profit of $40,000 is:**

A     $598,000

B     $651,000

C     $698,000

D     $706,000

**108** R Company provides a single service to its customers. An analysis of its budget for the year ending 31 December 20X5 shows that in period 3, when the budgeted activity was 6,570 service units with a sales value of $72 each, the margin of safety was 21.015%.

The budgeted contribution to sales ratio of the service is 35%.

**Budgeted fixed costs in period 3 were nearest to:**

A     $115,000

B     $131,000

C     $145,000

D     $157,000

**109** In order to utilise some spare capacity, K Ltd is preparing a quotation for a special order which requires 2,000 kgs of material J.

K Ltd has 800 kgs of material J in stock (original cost $7.00 per kg). Material J is used in the company's main product L. Each unit of L uses 5 kgs of material J and, based on an input value of $7.00 per kg of J, each unit of L yields a contribution of $10.00.

The resale value of material J is $5.50 per kg. The present replacement price of material J is $8.00 per kg. Material J is readily available in the market.

**The relevant cost of the 2,000 kgs of material J to be included in the quotation is $_____**

**110** **Which of the following are required to determine the breakeven sales value in a multi-product manufacturing environment?**

|  | Required? |
|---|---|
| The product-specific fixed costs |  |
| The product mix ratio |  |
| General fixed costs |  |
| The method of apportionment of general fixed costs |  |
| Individual product gross contribution to sales ratios |  |

**111** R Company currently sells products S, T and U in equal quantities and at the same selling price per unit. The contribution to sales ratio for product S is 60%; for product T it is 45% and the total is 52%. If fixed costs are unaffected by mix and are currently 25% of sales, the effect of changing the product mix to:

S    45%             T    20%             U    35%

**is that the total contribution/total sales ratio changes to:**

A    53.85%

B    52.00%

C    45.00%

D    33.33%

**112** EFG Company manufactures three products, which have the following cost and demand data:

|                                  | Product E | Product F | Product G |
| -------------------------------- | --------- | --------- | --------- |
| Contribution to sales ratio      | 30%       | 20%       | 25%       |
| Maximum sales value ($000)       | 1,200     | 1,400     | 1,900     |
| Minimum sales value ($000)       | 400       | 400       | 400       |

There are fixed costs of $850,000 per period.

**The lowest breakeven sales value per period, subject to meeting the minimum sales value constraints, is nearest to:**

A    $2,730,000

B    $2,840,000

C    $3,240,000

D    $3,400,000

**113** R Company manufactures and sells two products – S and T.  Annual sales are expected to be in the ratio of 3S : 5T.  Total annual sales are planned to be $640,000.  Product S has a contribution to sales ratio of 32% whereas that of product T is 48%.  Annual fixed costs are estimated to be $200,000.

**The margin of safety is __ _____% (round to one decimal place)**

**114** **A company provides three different levels of customer service support for one of its software products.**

The following data relate to these three levels of support:

| Support level | Superior<br>$ per contract | Standard<br>$ per contract | Basic<br>$ per contract |
|---|---|---|---|
| Annual fee | 1,000 | 750 | 400 |
| Annual variable costs | 450 | 250 | 180 |
| Annual fixed costs<br>(see note below) | 200 | 100 | 50 |
| Profit | 350 | 400 | 170 |

**Note:** The total annual fixed costs are budgeted to be $1,000,000. None of these costs are specific to any type of customer service support.

Assume that the number of customer service support contracts sold are in the proportion:

Superior 20%          Standard 30%                    Basic 50%

**The annual revenue that needs to be generated in order to break even is closest to:**

A      $1,690,000

B      $1,695,000

C      $1,710,000

D      $2,270,000

---

**The following data relates to Questions 115 and 116.**

R and K Company manufactures a product that has a selling price of $14 and variable costs of $6 per unit, and incurs annual fixed costs of $24,400. Annual sales demand is 8,000 units.

A new production method is currently under consideration that would increase fixed costs by 30%, but would reduce variable costs to $5 per unit. The superior quality of the finished product would enable sales to be increased to 8,500 units per annum at a price of $15 each.

---

**115** **If the change in production method were to take place, the breakeven output level would be:**

A      500 units higher

B      372 units higher

C      915 units higher

D      122 units higher

**116** **At what level of sales would the annual profit be the same with both production methods?**

A      3,660 units

B      4,280 units

C      4,960 units

D      3,172 units

---

117  XYZ Company sells three products.

Product X has a contribution to sales ratio of 40%.

Product Y has a contribution to sales ratio of 30%.

Product Z has a contribution to sales ratio of 35%.

Monthly fixed costs are $200,000.

The products are sold in the ratio:

X:3              Y:7              Z:5

**The monthly breakeven sales revenue is $_____ (round to the nearest to $000)**

118  A company has only a limited available supply of direct labour and direct materials. It manufactures two products, X and Y, for which there is unlimited sales demand at current selling prices. The resource requirements for each product are as follows:

|  | Product X | Product Y |
|---|---|---|
| Direct materials | 2 kg | 4 kg |
| Direct labour | 3 hours | 1 hour |

The company seeks to maximise its profits. Each unit of product X earns a contribution of $12 per unit.

**The minimum contribution that must be earned by a unit of product Y to make it worth producing units of product Y in a profit-maximising budget is $_____**

119  E Limited manufactures four products from different quantities of the same material which is in short supply.  The following budgeted data relates to the products:

|  | Product E1 $/unit | Product E2 $/unit | Product E3 $/unit | Product E4 $/unit |
|---|---|---|---|---|
| Selling price | 90 | 112 | 123 | 103 |
| Materials ($6 per kg) | 24 | 33 | 41 | 30 |
| Conversion costs | 40 | 65 | 65 | 55 |
|  | 64 | 98 | 106 | 85 |
| Profit | 26 | 14 | 17 | 18 |
| Machine time per unit in hours | 0.5 | 0.5 | 0.6 | 0.6 |

The conversion costs include general fixed costs that have been absorbed using a rate of $30 per machine hour.

**The ranking for the most profitable use of the raw materials is to make product:**

|  | 1st | 2nd | 3rd | 4th |
|---|---|---|---|---|
| A | E1 | E4 | E2 | E3 |
| B | E1 | E4 | E3 | E2 |
| C | E3 | E2 | E4 | E1 |
| D | E4 | E2 | E1 | E3 |

**120** **The shadow price of skilled labour for CBV Limited is currently $8 per hour. What does this mean?**

A    The cost of obtaining additional skilled labour resources is $8 per hour

B    There is a hidden cost of $8 for each hour of skilled labour actively worked

C    Contribution will be increased by $8 per hour for each extra hour of skilled labour that can be obtained

D    Total costs will be reduced by $8 for each additional hour of skilled labour that can be obtained

**121** P Limited is considering whether to continue making a component or buy it from an outside supplier.  It uses 12,000 of the components each year.

The internal manufacturing cost comprises:

|  | $/unit |
|---|---|
| Direct materials | 3.00 |
| Direct labour | 4.00 |
| Variable overhead | 1.00 |
| Specific fixed cost | 2.50 |
| Other fixed costs | 2.00 |
|  | 12.50 |

If the direct labour were not used to manufacture the component, it would be used to increase the production of another item for which there is unlimited demand.  This other item has a contribution of $10.00 per unit but requires $8.00 of labour per unit.

**The maximum price per component at which buying is preferable to internal manufacture is:**

A    $8.00

B    $10.50

C    $12.50

D    $15.50

122 Q plc makes two products – Quone and Qutwo – from the same raw material. The selling price and cost details of these products are as shown below:

|  | Quone | Qutwo |
|---|---|---|
|  | $ | $ |
| Selling price | 20.00 | 18.00 |
| Direct material ($2.00 per kg) | 6.00 | 5.00 |
| Direct labour | 4.00 | 3.00 |
| Variable overhead | 2.00 | 1.50 |
| Contribution per unit | 8.00 | 8.50 |

The maximum demand for these products is:

Quone             500 units per week

Qutwo            unlimited number of units per week

**If material were limited to 2,000 kgs per week, the shadow price of these materials would be:**

A     $nil

B     $2.00 per kg

C     $2.66 per kg

D     $3.40 per kg

123 The following details relate to three services provided by RST Company:

|  | Service R | Service S | Service T |
|---|---|---|---|
|  | $ | $ | $ |
| Fee charged to customers | 100 | 150 | 160 |
| Unit service costs: |  |  |  |
| Direct materials | 15 | 30 | 25 |
| Direct labour | 20 | 35 | 30 |
| Variable overhead | 15 | 20 | 22 |
| Fixed overhead | 25 | 50 | 50 |

All three services use the same type of direct labour which is paid $25 per hour.

The fixed overheads are general fixed overheads that have been absorbed on the basis of machine hours.

**If direct labour is a scarce resource, the most and least profitable uses of it are:**

|  | Most profitable | Least profitable |
|---|---|---|
| A | S | R |
| B | S | T |
| C | T | R |
| D | T | S |

**124** BJS Company uses three components, P, Q and R, in its main product. The budget for next year indicates a requirement for 3,000 of each component. The components are all manufactured on the same machine, for which only 50,000 hours are available next year. The variable cost of internal manufacture of each component together with the machine hours used are shown in the table below. The table also shows prices quoted by a sub-contractor for supplying the components.

| Component | Machine hours per unit | Variable cost $ per unit | Sub-contractor $ per unit |
|---|---|---|---|
| P | 9 | 45 | 65 |
| Q | 5 | 70 | 78 |
| R | 12 | 56 | 80 |

**The minimum total cost (to the nearest $000) at which BJS Company can obtain the full requirement of components is $_____**

**125** A company manufactures a range of products one of which, product L, incurs a total cost of $60 per unit.

The company manufactures 50,000 units each year and the directors wish to achieve a return of 15% on the total capital of $10,000,000 invested in the company.

**Based on this information the cost-plus selling price (to the nearest $) of one unit of product L should be $_____**

**126** JK manufactures a product with the following standard information:

| | $/unit |
|---|---|
| Direct materials | 9.00 |
| Direct labour | 14.00 |
| Total direct cost | 23.00 |

Additional information on the product is provided as follows:

| | |
|---|---|
| Direct labour hours per unit | 2 hours |
| Production overhead absorption rate | $4.50 per direct labour hour |
| Mark-up for non-production overhead costs | 10% of total production costs |
| Required return on sales revenue | 20% |

**The target selling price for the product will be:**

A $27.60

B $40.00

C $42.24

D $44.00

**127** The following equations have been taken from the plans of DX for the year ending 31 December 20X5:

Contribution (in dollars) = 12 X1 + 5 X2 + 8 X3

Materials: 2 X1 + 3 X2 + 4 X3 = 12,000 kilos

Machine hours: 6 X1 + 4 X2 + 3 X3 = 8,000 machine hours

$0 \leq X1 \leq 2,000$

$100 \leq X2 \leq 500$

$0 \leq X3 \leq 200$

where: X1, X2, and X3 are the number of units of products produced and sold,

**If an unlimited supply of raw material could be obtained at the current price, the product mix that maximises the value of DX plc's contribution is:**

|   | X1 | X2 | X3 |
|---|---|---|---|
| A | 1,333 | 0 | 0 |
| B | 1,233 | 0 | 200 |
| C | 1,166 | 100 | 200 |
| D | 1,241 | 100 | 50 |

**128** The budgeted profit statement for Product X for next year shows that it has a margin of safety equal to 20% of budgeted sales and a unit selling price of $10. Product X has a contribution to sales (c/s) ratio of 60% and budgeted fixed costs of $120,000 for the year.

**The percentage increase in the unit variable cost that would result in Product X breaking even at the budgeted level of activity is _____%**

**129** A factory's entire machine capacity is used to produce essential components. The costs of using the machines are as follows:

|   | $ |
|---|---|
| Variable costs | 15,000 |
| Fixed costs | 50,000 |
|   | ――― |
|   | 65,000 |
|   | ――― |

If all the components are purchased from an outside supplier, the machines could be used to produce other items which would earn a total contribution of $25,000.

**The maximum price that a profit-maximising company should be willing to pay to the outside supplier for the components is $_____**

**130** The following details relate to ready meals that are prepared by a food processing company:

| Ready meal | K $/meal | L $/meal | M $/meal |
|---|---|---|---|
| Selling price | 5.00 | 3.00 | 4.40 |
| Ingredients | 2.00 | 1.00 | 1.30 |
| Variable conversion costs | 1.60 | 0.80 | 1.85 |
| Fixed conversion costs* | 0.50 | 0.30 | 0.60 |
| Profit | 0.90 | 0.90 | 0.65 |
| Oven time (minutes per ready meal) | 10 | 4 | 8 |

*The fixed conversion costs are general fixed costs that are not specific to any type of ready meal.

Each of the meals is prepared using a series of processes, one of which involves cooking the ingredients in a large oven. The availability of cooking time in the oven is limited and, because each of the meals requires cooking at a different oven temperature, it is not possible to cook more than one of the meals in the oven at the same time.

**The most and least profitable use of the oven is: (fill in the letter for the most and least profitable meal)**

| | Meal? |
|---|---|
| Most profitable | |
| Least profitable | |

**131** **Which of the following are limitations of the linear programming technique?**

| | Limitation? |
|---|---|
| Linear relationships must exist | |
| There can only be two products | |
| There can only be two scarce resources | |
| All variables must be completely divisible | |
| A computer must be used to find the optimal point | |

**132** The standard output from a joint process was 5,000 litres of Product K, 3,000 litres of Product L and 2,000 litres of Product M. The total cost of the joint process was $156,000. The company is now deciding if it should modify Product K by putting it through an additional process.

**In order to help with that decision the best way to apportion the joint costs of $156,000 to the products is:**

A     in the ratio of 5 : 3 : 2

B     in the ratio of the sales value at the split off point

C     in the ratio of the sales value after further processing

D     none of the above method

**133** An organization has created the following linear programming solution to represent the position it faces currently in the presence of short term scarce resources:

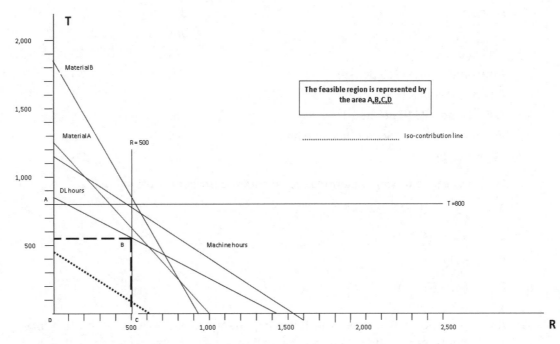

Note: DL = Direct labour hours

The point marked P has been determined to be the point which provides the optimal production plan.

**Which of the following resources will have a shadow price greater than 0? (tick all that apply)**

| | Shadow price >0? |
|---|---|
| Direct labour hours | |
| Material A | |
| Material B | |
| Machine hours | |

**134** JRL manufactures two products from different combinations of the same resources. Unit selling prices and unit cost details for each product are as follows:

| Product | J | L |
|---|---|---|
| | $/unit | $/unit |
| Selling price | 115 | 120 |
| Direct material A ($10 per kg) | 20 | 10 |
| Direct material B ($6 per kg) | 12 | 24 |
| Skilled labour ($14 per hour) | 28 | 21 |
| Variable overhead ($4 per machine hour) | 14 | 18 |
| Fixed overhead | 28 | 36 |

**Which of the following equations represents the iso-contribution line?**

A    13J + 11L = M

B    41J + 47L = M

C    54J + 58L = M

D    54J + 65L = M

**135** An organization has created the following linear programming solution to represent the position it faces currently in the presence of short term scarce resources:

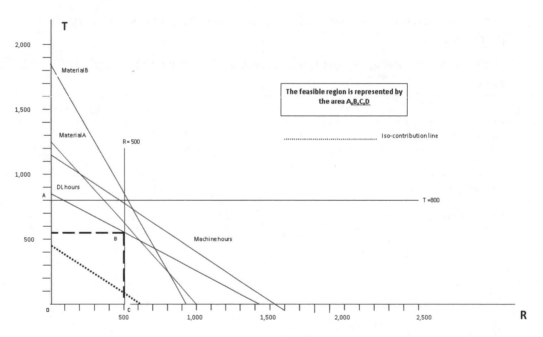

The organisation manufactures two products, T and R. Each T requires 4kgs of material A and each R requires 2kgs of material A.

**The maximum amount of Material A available is _____ kgs**

## BUDGETING

136 Which of the following can be identified as purposes of budgeting (*tick all that apply*)?

|  | *Purpose of budgeting?* |
|---|---|
| Communication |  |
| Authorisation |  |
| Sales maximisation |  |
| Co-ordination |  |

**The following data relate to Questions 137 and 138.**

A division of LMN operates a fleet of minibuses that carries people and packages for other divisions.

In the year ended 31 October 20X3, it carried 4,420 people and 30,500 kgs of packages. It incurred costs of $850,000.

The division has found that 60% of its total costs are variable, and that 50% of these vary with the number of people and the other 50% varies with the weight of the packages.

The company is now preparing its budget for the three months ending 31 January 20X4 using an incremental budgeting approach. In this period it expects:

- All prices to be 2% higher than the average paid in the year ended 31 October 20X3.

- Efficiency levels to be unchanged.

- Activity levels to be:

    - 1,150 people

    - 8,100 kgs of packages.

137 The budgeted people-related cost (to the nearest $100) for the three months ending 31 January 20X4 is:

A $55,300

B $6,400

C $66,300

D $67,700

138 The budgeted package-related cost (to the nearest $100) for the three months ending 31 January 20X4 is:

A $56,400

B $57,600

C $67,800

D $69,000

**139** EFG uses an Activity Based Budgeting system. It manufactures three products, budgeted details of which are set out below:

|  | Product E | Product F | Product G |
|---|---|---|---|
| Budgeted annual production (units) | 75,000 | 120,000 | 60,000 |
| Batch size (units) | 200 | 60 | 30 |
| Machine set-ups per batch | 5 | 3 | 9 |

Three cost pools have been identified. Budgeted machine set-up costs for the year are $180,000.

**The budgeted machine set-up cost per unit of product F is $_____**

**140** The following details relate to product X in two accounting periods:

| Number of units | 500 | 800 |
|---|---|---|
|  | $/unit | $/unit |
| Direct materials | 2.00 | 2.00 |
| Direct labour | 1.50 | 1.50 |
| Production overhead | 2.50 | 1.75 |
| Other overhead | 1.00 | 0.625 |
|  | 7.00 | 5.875 |

**The fixed cost per period and variable cost per unit are:**

|  | Period fixed cost | Variable cost/unit |
|---|---|---|
|  | $ | $ |
| A | 1,000 | 1.125 |
| B | 1,000 | 4.00 |
| C | 1,500 | 3.50 |
| D | 1,500 | 4.00 |

**141** PP Ltd is preparing the production and material purchases budgets for one of their products, the SUPERX, for the forthcoming year.

The following information is available:

SUPERX

| Sales demand (units) | 30,000 |
|---|---|
| Material usage per unit | 7 kgs |
| Estimated opening inventory | 3,500 units |
| Required closing inventory | 35% higher than opening inventory |

**How many units of the SUPERX will need to be produced?**

A  28,775

B  30,000

C  31,225

D  38,225

**142** **An incremental budgeting system is:**

A    a system which budgets only for the extra costs associated with a particular plan

B    a system which budgets for the variable manufacturing costs only

C    a system which prepares budgets only after the manager responsible has justified the continuation of the relevant activity

D    a system which prepares budgets by adjusting the previous year's values by expected changes in volumes of activity and price/inflation effects

**143**    A company has the following expected sales for the next three months of the year:

| April | 12,000 units |
|---|---|
| May | 15,000 units |
| June | 18,000 units |

The opening inventory of the product in April is expected to be 3,600 units.

At the end of each month closing inventory is expected to equal 30% of the following month's sales

**The expected level of production in May is _____ units**

**144**    The following cost per unit details have been extracted from a production overhead cost budget:

| Output (units) | 6,000 | 10,000 |
|---|---|---|
| Production overhead ($/unit) | 3.20 | 3.00 |

**The budget cost allowance for production overhead for an activity level of 7,350 units is:**

A    $20,505

B    $21,765

C    $22,845

D    $23,515

**145**    **H is forecasting its sales for next year using a combination of time series and regression analysis models. An analysis of past sales units has produced the following equation for the quarterly sales trend:**

$y = 26x + 8,850$

where the value of x represents the quarterly accounting period and the value of y represents the quarterly sales trend in units. Quarter 1 of next year will have a value for x of 25.

The quarterly seasonal variations have been measured using the multiplicative (proportional) model and are:

| Quarter 1 | − 15% |
|---|---|
| Quarter 2 | − 5% |
| Quarter 3 | + 5% |
| Quarter 4 | + 15% |

Production is planned to occur at a constant rate throughout the year.

The company does not hold inventories at the end of any year.

**The difference between the budgeted sales for quarter 1 and quarter 4 next year are:**

A      78 units

B      2,850 units

C      2,862 units

D      2,940 units

**146** **Which of the following definitions best describes 'Zero-Based Budgeting'?**

A      A method of budgeting where an attempt is made to make the expenditure under each cost heading as close to zero as possible.

B      A method of budgeting whereby all activities are re-evaluated each time a budget is formulated.

C      A method of budgeting that recognises the difference between the behaviour of fixed and variable costs with respect to changes in output and the budget is designed to change appropriately with such fluctuations.

D      A method of budgeting where the sum of revenues and expenditures in each budget centre must equal zero.

**147** The overhead costs of RP have been found to be accurately represented by the formula:

$$y = \$10,000 + \$0.25x$$

where y is the monthly cost and x represents the activity level measured as the number of orders.

Monthly activity levels of orders may be estimated using a combined regression analysis and time series model:

$$a = 100,000 + 30b$$

where a represents the de-seasonalised monthly activity level and b represents the month number.

In month 240, the seasonal index value is 108.

**The overhead cost for RP for month 240 is $_____ (round to the nearest $1,000)**

**148** Monthly sales of product R follow a linear trend of $y = 9.72 + 5.816x$, where y is the number of units sold and x is the number of the month. Monthly deviations from the trend follow an additive model.

**The forecast number of units of product R to be sold in month 23, which has a seasonal factor of plus 6.5 is, to the nearest whole unit:**

A      134

B      137

C      143

D      150

**149** Nile is preparing its sales budget . Estimated sales are 120,000 units if the Summer is rainy, and 80,000 units if the Summer is dry. The probability of a dry Summer is 0.4.

**What is the expected value for sales volume?**

A   96,000 units

B   100,000 units

C   104,000 units

D   120,000 units

**150** The budgeted total costs for two levels of output are as shown below:

| Output | 25,000 units | 40,000 units |
|---|---|---|
| Total cost | $143,500 | $194,000 |

Within this range of output it is known that the variable cost per unit is constant but fixed costs rise by $10,000 when output exceeds 35,000 units.

**The total fixed costs for a budgeted output of 36,000 units are $_____**

**151** **Which of the following best describes 'budgetary slack'?**

A   The difference between what has been set as a budgetary objective and what has been achieved for the period

B   The demotivating impact of a budgetary target that has been set too high

C   The deliberate over-estimation of expenditure and/or under-estimation of revenues in the budgetary planning process

D   Accumulated favourable variances reported against a specific item of budgeted expenditure

**152** Z plc has found that it can estimate future sales using time series analysis and regression techniques.  The following trend equation has been derived:

$$y = 25,000 + 6,500x$$

where

y is the total sales units per quarter

x is the time period reference number

Z has also derived the following set of seasonal variation index values for each quarter using a multiplicative (proportional) model:

| Quarter 1 | 70 |
|---|---|
| Quarter 2 | 90 |
| Quarter 3 | 150 |
| Quarter 4 | 90 |

**Assuming that the first quarter of year 1 is time period reference number 1, the forecast for sales units for the third quarter of year 7, is _____ units**

**153** A company is preparing its maintenance budget. The number of machine hours and maintenance costs for the past six months have been as follows:

| Month | Machine hours | $ |
|---|---|---|
| 1 | 10,364 | 35,319 |
| 2 | 12,212 | 39,477 |
| 3 | 8,631 | 31,420 |
| 4 | 9,460 | 33,285 |
| 5 | 8,480 | 31,080 |
| 6 | 10,126 | 34,784 |

The budget cost allowance for an activity level of 9,340 machine hours, before any adjustment for price changes, is nearest to:

A    $21,000

B    $30,200

C    $33,000

D    $34,000

**154** MM is preparing its cash budget for February using the following data.

One line in the cash budget is for purchases of a raw material, J. The opening inventory of J in January is expected to be 1,075 units. The price of J is expected to be $8 per unit. The company pays for purchases at the end of the month following delivery.

Production is expected to be 4,300 units in January and 5,300 units in February and each production unit uses one unit of material J.

At the end of each month raw materials inventory is expected to be 25% of the requirement for the following month's production

The value for purchases of J to be included in the cash budget for February is $_____

**155** If the budgeted fixed costs increase, the gradient of the line plotted on the budgeted Profit/Volume (P/V) chart will:

A    increase

B    decrease

C    not change

D    become curvi-linear

**156** A master budget comprises the:

A    budgeted income statement and budgeted cash flow only.

B    budgeted income statement and budgeted balance sheet only.

C    budgeted income statement and budgeted capital expenditure only.

D    budgeted income statement, budgeted balance sheet and budgeted cash flow only.

**157**  K has determined a cost driver rate for quality testing as $850 per test.

During the year there were actually on average 50 tests per month, giving a variance on the total cost for quality testing of $102,000 for the year.

**The budgeted cost per month for quality testing is $_____**

**158**  D plc operates a retail business. Purchases are sold at cost plus 25%. The management team is preparing the cash budget and has gathered the following data:

1    The budgeted sales are as follows:

| Month | $000 |
|---|---|
| July | 100 |
| August | 90 |
| September | 125 |

2    It is management policy to hold inventory at the end of each month which is sufficient to meet sales demand in the next half month. Sales are budgeted to occur evenly during each month.

3    Creditors are paid one month after the purchase has been made.

**The entry for 'purchases' that will be shown in the cash budget for August is $_____**

**159**  XYZ Ltd is preparing the production budget for the next period. The total costs of production are a semi-variable cost. The following cost information has been collected in connection with production:

| Volume (units) | Cost |
|---|---|
| 4,500 | $29,000 |
| 6,500 | $33,000 |

**The estimated total production costs for a production volume of 5,750 units is nearest to**

A    $29,200

B    $30,000

C    $31,500

D    $32,500

**160**  S plc produces and sells three products, X, Y and Z. It has contracts to supply products X and Y, which will utilise all of the specific materials that are available to make these two products during the next period. The revenue these contracts will generate and the contribution to sales (C/S) ratios of products X and Y are as follows:

|  | Product X | Product Y |
|---|---|---|
| Revenue | $10 million | $20 million |
| C/S ratio | 15% | 10% |

Product Z has a C/S ratio of 25%.

The total fixed costs of S plc are $5.5 million during the next period and management has budgeted to earn a profit of $2 million.

**The revenue that needs to be generated by Product Z for S plc to achieve the budgeted profit is $_____ million**

**161**   A company has the following budgeted sales figures:

Month 1     $105,000
Month 2     $120,000
Month 3     $108,000

80% of sales are on credit and the remainder are paid in cash. Credit customers paying within one month are given a discount of 1.5%. Credit customers normally pay within the following time frame:

Within 1 month     40% of credit sales

Within 2 months    98% of credit sales

There is an expectation that 2% of credit sales will become irrecoverable (bad) debts.

Outstanding receivables at the beginning of month 1 includes $6,000 expected to be received in month 3.

**The total receipts expected in month 3 are $_____**

**162**   CJD Ltd manufactures plastic components for the car industry. The following budgeted information is available for three of its key plastic components:

|  | W | X | Y |
|---|---|---|---|
|  | $ per unit | $ per unit | $ per unit |
| Selling price | 200 | 183 | 175 |
| Direct material | 50 | 40 | 35 |
| Direct labour | 30 | 35 | 30 |
| Units produced and sold | 10,000 | 15,000 | 18,000 |

The total number of activities for each of the three products for the period is as follows:

|  | | | |
|---|---|---|---|
| Number of purchase requisitions | 1,200 | 1,800 | 2,000 |
| Number of set ups | 240 | 260 | 300 |

Overhead costs have been analysed as follows:

| | |
|---|---|
| Receiving/inspecting quality assurance | $1,400,000 |
| Production scheduling/machine set up | $1,200,000 |

**The budgeted profit per unit for Product X using activity-based budgeting is $_____**

**163**   GS has budgeted sales for the next two years of 24,000 units per annum spread evenly throughout both years. The estimated opening inventory of finished goods at the start of the next year is 500 units but GS now wants to maintain inventory of finished goods equivalent to one month's sales.

Each unit uses 2 kg of material. The estimated opening raw material inventory at the start of the next year is 300 kg but GS now wants to hold sufficient raw material inventory at the end of each month to cover the following month's production.

The change in the policy for inventory holding for both raw materials and finished goods will take effect in the first month of next year and will apply for the next two years.

The budgeted material cost is $12 per kg.

**The  material purchases budget for the next year is $_____**

**164** JB has budgeted production for the next budget year of 36,000 units. Each unit of production requires 4 labour hours and the budgeted labour rate is $12 per hour excluding overtime. Idle time is expected to be 10% of total hours available i.e. including idle time. Due to labour shortages it is expected that 20% of the hours paid, including idle time, will be paid at an overtime rate of time and a half.

**The labour cost budget for the year is $_____**

**165** A company is preparing its annual budget and is estimating the number of units of Product A that it will sell in each quarter of Year 2. Past experience has shown that the trend for sales of the product is represented by the following relationship:

y = a + bx where

y = number of sales units in the quarter

a = 10,000 units

b = 3,000 units

x = the quarter number where 1 = quarter 1 of Year 1

Actual sales of Product A in Year 1 were affected by seasonal variations and were as follows:

Quarter 1:    14,000 units

Quarter 2:    18,000 units

Quarter 3:    18,000 units

Quarter 4:    20,000 units

**Using the additive model, after adjusting for seasonal variations, the expected sales of Product A for Quarter 3 of Year 2 is _____ units**

**166** AB is preparing its cash budget for next year. The accounts receivable at the beginning of next year are expected to be $460,000. The budgeted sales are $5,400,000 and will occur evenly throughout the year. 80% of the budgeted sales will be on credit and the remainder will be cash sales. Credit customers pay in the month following sale.

**The budgeted cash receipts from customers next year are:**

A    $5,040,000

B    $5,410,000

C    $5,500,000

D    $5,890,000

**167** B's latest estimate for trade payables outstanding at the end of this year is 45 days. Estimated purchases for this year are $474,500. DB is preparing the budget for next year and estimates that purchases will increase by 10%.

The trade payables amount, in $, outstanding at the end of next year is estimated to be the same as at the end of this year.

**The budgeted trade payable days at the end of next year are _____ days *(round to the nearest whole day)***

**168** AB is preparing its purchases budget for raw material C for the forthcoming year. The opening inventory of raw material C is expected to be 2,000 kg and the price is expected to be $8 per kg.

Raw material C is used only in the production of Product D. Each unit of Product D requires two kg of material C. Budgeted sales of Product D for the forthcoming year and for the following year are 36,000 units in each year. Sales will occur evenly throughout each year. The opening inventory is expected to be 6,000 units.

AB will implement a new inventory policy from the first month of the forthcoming year. The closing inventory that will be required at the end of the forthcoming year is as follows:

Raw material inventory: one month's production requirements

Finished goods inventory: one month's sales requirements

**The material purchases budget for the forthcoming year is $_____**

**169** PJ has budgeted sales for the next two years of 144,000 units per annum spread evenly throughout each year. The estimated closing inventory at the end of this year is 6,500 units. PJ wants to change its inventory policy so that it holds inventory equivalent to one month's sales. The change in inventory policy will take place at the beginning of next year and will apply for the next two years.

Each unit produced requires 2 hours of direct labour. The budgeted direct labour rate per hour is $15. It is anticipated that 80% of production will be paid at the budgeted rate and the remainder will be paid at the overtime rate of time and a half. PJ treats overtime costs as part of direct labour costs.

**The direct labour cost budget for the next year is $_____**

**170** The following budgeted information comes from the accounting records of Ross

| Production units | 1,000 | 2,000 | 3,000 |
|---|---|---|---|
| | $ | $ | $ |
| Material cost | 15,000 | 30,000 | 45,000 |
| Labour cost | 10,000 | 20,000 | 30,000 |
| Overhead cost | 18,000 | 22,000 | 26,000 |
| Distribution cost | 12,000 | 12,000 | 12,000 |
| | | | |
| Total cost | 55,000 | 84,000 | 113,000 |

**What would be the budgeted cost for 2,750 units?**

A    $103,583

B    $105,750

C    $106,750

D    $109,250

**The following data relate to Questions 171 and 172.**

A company is estimating its costs based on past information. The total costs incurred by the company at different levels of output were as follows:

| Output (units) | Total costs $ |
|---|---|
| 160,000 | 2,420,000 |
| 185,000 | 2,775,000 |
| 190,000 | 2,840,000 |

The company uses the high-low method to separate total costs into their fixed and variable elements. Ignore inflation.

171   **The estimated total costs for an output of 205,000 units is:**

A   $2,870,000

B   $3,050,000

C   $3,064,211

D   $3,080,857

172   The company has now established that there is a stepped increase in fixed costs of $30,000 when output reaches 180,000 units.

**The estimate of total costs for an output of 175,000 units using the additional information is:**

A   $2,645,000

B   $2,275,000

C   $2,615,000

D   $2,630,000

173   Murray had the following budget and actual results during a period:

|  | Original budget | Actual |
|---|---|---|
| Sales units | 1,000 | 1,380 |
|  | $ | $ |
| Sales revenue | 100,000 | 133,860 |
| Direct material | 40,000 | 57,800 |
| Direct labour | 20,000 | 27,000 |
| Variable overhead | 15,000 | 18,600 |
| Fixed overhead | 10,000 | 11,000 |
| Profit | 15,000 | 19,460 |

**Using a flexed budget approach, the total adverse profit variance for the period is $_____**

**The following data relate to Questions 174 and 175.**

A company is estimating future sales using time-series analysis. The following trend equation has been derived from actual sales data for Year 1:

y = 22,000 + 800x

where      y is the total sales units for the quarter, and

              x is the time period (Quarter 1 of Year 1 is time period 1)

The following set of seasonal variation index values has been derived using a multiplicative model and based on Year 1 actual sales:

| | |
|---|---|
| Quarter 1 | 70 |
| Quarter 2 | 90 |
| Quarter 3 | 130 |
| Quarter 4 | 110 |

**174** **Using the above multiplicative time series model, sales for Year 2 Quarter 3 would be estimated as:**

     A      35,880 units

     B      40,040 units

     C      27,600 units

     D      27,730 units

**175** **Using an additive time series model, the amount of the seasonal variation for Quarter 2 would be:**

     A      − 2,680

     B      − 2,360

     C      + 2,680

     D      + 2,360

**176**      D plc operates a retail business. Purchases are sold at cost plus 25%. The management team is preparing the cash budget and has gathered the following data:

     1      The budgeted sales are as follows:

| Month | $000 |
|---|---|
| August | 90 |
| September | 125 |
| October | 140 |

     2      It is management policy to hold inventory at the end of each month which is sufficient to meet sales demand in the next half month. Sales are budgeted to occur evenly during each month.

     3      Creditors are paid one month after the purchase has been made.

**The entry for 'purchases' that will be shown in the cash budget for September is $_____**

**177** AB is preparing its cash budget for next year. The estimated accounts payable balance at the beginning of next year is $540,000. The budgeted purchases for next year are $6,800,000, occurring evenly throughout the year. It is estimated that 75% of purchases will be on credit and the remainder will be for cash. The company pays for credit purchases in the month following purchase.

**The budgeted cash payments to suppliers next year are:**

A    $6,375,000

B    $6,773,333

C    $6,915,000

D    $5,215,000

**178** The following costs have been estimated for the following period.

| | |
|---|---|
| Direct material | $20,000 |
| Electricity | $8,750 |
| Indirect labour | $37,500 |
| Rent | $6,000 |
| Royalty fee | $2,150 |

**What would be the total overhead budget for the period?**

A    $74,000

B    $72,250

C    $52,250

D    $14,750

**179** **Match the following costs to the correct budget (draw a line connecting the cost to the correct budget)**

| Cost |
|---|
| Commission paid to an agent for selling the product |
| Electricity used in the factory |
| Depreciation of factory building |
| Packaging material to protect the product |

| Budget |
|---|
| Distribution overhead budget |
| Variable production overhead budget |
| Selling overhead budget |
| Fixed production overhead budget |

**180** The following budgeted information comes from the accounting records of Ross Ltd

| | | |
|---|---|---|
| Production units | 1,000 | 2,000 |
| Budgeted cost | $18,000 | $24,000 |

**What would be the budgeted cost for 1,980 units?**

A    $19,680

B    $21,480

C    $23,880

D    $24,280

**181** During a period, A Ltd expected to produce 5,000 units using 16,000 labour hours and 9,000 machine hours.

**If the budgeted overhead absorption rate was $12.50 per labour hour, the budgeted fixed overheads in the period were $_____**

**182** The following budgeted information comes from the accounting records of ABC

|  | Product A | Product B |
|---|---|---|
| Production units | 1,000 | 2,000 |
| Labour hours per unit | 0.5 hours | 2 hours |
| Machine hours per unit | 0.25 hours | 1.5 hours |
| Variable overhead rate (per machine hour) | $1.50 per hour | |
| Fixed overhead rate (per labour hour) | $1.95 per hour | |

**What would be the total overhead budget for the period?**

A   $11,625

B   $13,088

C   $13,650

D   $15,113

**183** **Which of the following would be included in the fixed production overhead budget?**

A   The annual salary of a supervisor that monitors the performance of factory workers

B   The annual rent charged on the head office building

C   The annual variable electricity usage charge of the factory machinery used to make the product

D   The annual cost of materials used to make the product

**184** **A flexible budget is best defined as**

A   A budget for a single level of activity that does not change in a period

B   A budget that is based on zero expenditure and is only increased if the expenditure is fully justified

C   A budget for the number of units that were actually sold during a period

D   A budget that can be restated to any level of output

**185** **Which TWO of the following are not criticisms of incremental budgeting?**

|  | Not a criticism? |
|---|---|
| It may make managers, staff and unions feel threatened | |
| It encourages slack | |
| It is time consuming as it involves starting from scratch | |
| It encourages wasteful spending | |
| It includes past inefficiencies as costs are not scrutinised | |

**186** The following budgeted information comes from the accounting records of Smith

|  | *Original budget* |
|---|---|
| Sales units | 1,000 |
|  | $ |
| Sales revenue | 100,000 |
| Direct material | 40,000 |
| Direct labour | 20,000 |
| Variable overhead | 15,000 |
| Fixed overhead | 10,000 |
| Profit | 15,000 |

**In a period where the actual sales were 1,200 units, what would be the flexed budget?**

A      $17,000

B      $20,000

C      $22,000

D      $35,000

**187** **Which two of the following are not characteristics of rolling budgets?**

|  | *Characteristic of rolling budgets?* |
|---|---|
| Budgets are more likely to be realistic as there is a shorter period between preparation and actual events occurring |  |
| Updates to budgets are only made when they are foreseeable |  |
| They reduce uncertainty in budgeting |  |
| They force management to look ahead more frequently |  |
| Each item of expenditure must be fully justified before inclusion in the budget |  |

**188** **Which one of the following best describes incremental budgeting?**

A      Increments of income and expenditure are compared with forecasted results

B      A method of budgeting where all activities are re-evaluated each time a budget is formulated

C      A budget updated in regular increments by adding a further accounting period when the earliest period has expired

D      The budget for each period is based on prior period results, modified for changes in activity levels

**189** **The following is a description of which method of budgeting?**

'A budget continuously updated by adding a further accounting period when the earliest accounting period has expired.'

A    Zero based budgeting

B    Activity based budgeting

C    Incremental budgeting

D    Rolling budgets

**190** RF has prepared the following sales forecast for its first three months of trading:

| Month | Number of components |
|-------|----------------------|
| 1 | 1,500 |
| 2 | 1,750 |
| 3 | 2,000 |

The selling price has been set at $10 per component in the first three months.

**Sales receipts**

| Time of payment | % of customers |
|-----------------|----------------|
| Month of sale | 20* |
| One month later | 45 |
| Two months later | 25 |
| Three months later | 5 |

The balance represents anticipated bad debts.

*A 2% discount is given to customers for payment received in the month of sale.

**The sales receipts for month 2 are budgeted to be $_____**

**191** LF has the following expected production for the next three months:

| Month | 1 | 2 | 3 |
|-------|------|------|------|
| | units | units | units |
| Production | 1,850 | 1,800 | 2,020 |

The variable production overhead cost per unit is $1.20. 60% of these will be paid in the month in which production occurs and the remainder will be paid one month later.

**What will be the variable overhead payment in month 2?**

A    $2,160

B    $2,424

C    $1,296

D    $2,184

192    Which of the following best describes Zero Based Budgeting (ZBB)?

   A    A method of budgeting where all activities are re-evaluated each time a budget is formulated

   B    A method of budgeting that tries to make expenditure as close to zero as possible

   C    method of budgeting where the sum of all costs and revenues must be zero

   D    A budget that has zero variance between forecast and actual results

193    Which two of the following are limitations of 'what if' analysis in cash budgeting?

| | Limitations of 'What if' analysis? |
|---|---|
| Only one variable changes at a time | |
| It assesses the risk to the closing cash balance | |
| It provides an assessment of how responsive the cash flows are to changes in variables | |
| Probabilities of changes are not accounted for | |
| It directs attention to critical variables | |

# THE TREATMENT OF UNCERTAINTY IN DECISION MAKING

194    The daily demand for a perishable product has the following probability distribution:

| Demand (units) | Probability |
|---|---|
| 100 | 0.25 |
| 200 | 0.40 |
| 300 | 0.35 |

Each item costs $4 and is sold for $8.  Unsold items are thrown away at the end of the day.

**If orders must be placed before the daily demand is known, the number of  units that should be purchased at the beginning of each day in order to maximise expected profit is _____ units**

195    A company has estimated the selling prices and variable costs of one of its products as follows:

| Selling price per unit | | Variable cost per unit | |
|---|---|---|---|
| $ | Probability | $ | Probability |
| 40 | 0.30 | 20 | 0.55 |
| 50 | 0.45 | 30 | 0.25 |
| 60 | 0.25 | 40 | 0.20 |

The company will be able to supply 1,000 units of its product each week irrespective of the selling price. Selling price and variable cost per unit are independent of each other.

**The probability that the weekly contribution will exceed $20,000 is _____% (round to the nearest whole %)**

**The following data relate to Questions 196 and 197.**

X Company can choose from five mutually exclusive projects. The projects will each last for one year only and their net cash inflows will be determined by the prevailing market conditions. The forecast annual cash inflows and their associated probabilities are shown below.

| Market conditions | Poor | Good | Excellent |
|---|---|---|---|
| Probability | 0.20 | 0.50 | 0.30 |
| | $000 | $000 | $000 |
| Project L | 500 | 470 | 550 |
| Project M | 400 | 550 | 570 |
| Project N | 450 | 400 | 475 |
| Project O | 360 | 400 | 420 |
| Project P | 600 | 500 | 425 |

196  Based on the expected value of the net cash inflows, which project should be undertaken?

    A    L

    B    M

    C    N

    D    P

197  The value of perfect information about the state of the market is:

    A    Nil

    B    $5,000

    C    $26,000

    D    $40,000

198  A baker is trying to decide the number of batches of a particular type of bread that he should bake each day. Daily demand ranges from 10 batches to 12 batches. Each batch of bread that is baked and sold yields a positive contribution of $50, but each batch of bread baked that is not sold yields a negative contribution of $20.

    Assuming the baker adopts the *minimax regret* decision rule, the number of batches of bread that he should bake each day is _____ batches

199  Match the decision criterion with the assumed approach to risk taken by the decision maker *(draw a line connecting the decision criteria to the correct attitude to risk)*

| Decision criteria |
|---|
| Expected values |
| Maximax |
| Maximin |
| Minimax regret |

| Attitude to risk |
|---|
| Risk averse |
| Risk averse |
| Riske neutral |
| Risk seeker |

**200** A company is making a decision on whether to launch a new product. The decision is illustrated in the following decision tree:

Profit outcome

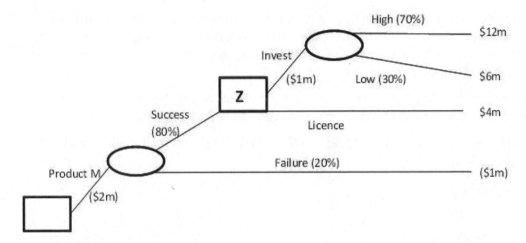

The profit outcomes do not include the cost of any investments made.

The expected value at point Z is $9.2m.

**What is the overall expected value from the product launch?**

A     $5.16m

B     $7.16m

C     $7.36m

D     $9.20m

**201** Chris orders bunches of flowers from a wholesaler which he then sells on his market stall. Chris has to order the flowers before the demand is known, any unsold flowers are thrown away at the end of the day.

A payoff table below shows the profits Chris can expect based upon the quantity he orders and the level of demand.

| Demand | Order level | | | |
|---|---|---|---|---|
|  | 20 bunches | 30 bunches | 40 bunches | 50 bunches |
| 20 bunches | $60 | $20 | $(20) | $(60) |
| 30 bunches | $60 | $90 | $50 | $10 |
| 40 bunches | $60 | $90 | $120 | $80 |
| 50 bunches | $60 | $90 | $120 | $150 |

**Using a minimax regret table, the order level that would be selected if Chris applied the minimax regret decision criterion is:**

A     20 bunches

B     30 bunches

C     40 bunches

D     50 bunches

202 Soggy makes paddling pools and has to decide in advance how many pools to make before the summer demand is known. Demand is determined by the weather, if it is very hot and sunny demand will be high, if it is a rainy cold summer demand will be low and a warm summer will result in average demand.

The budgeted profit for the current year is $1,190,000. The profit for the previous year was very low due to a wet summer so Soggy is considering employing the services of a meteorologist to predict the likely weather for this summer. The predictions are not perfect but should give a good indication.

Soggy has decided that it is prepared to pay a maximum of $30,000 for the meteorologist services as using the predictions should result in an expected profit of $1,250,000.

**What is the expected profit for Soggy Ltd if the meteorologist had not been employed?**

A       $1,280,000

B       $1,250,000

C       $1,220,000

D       $1,190,000

---

**The following data relate to Questions 203 and 204.**

P Company currently sells 90,000 units of product Y per annum.  At this level of sales and output, the selling price and variable cost per unit are $50 and $21 respectively.  The annual fixed costs are $1,200,000.  The management team is considering lowering the selling price per unit to $45.

The estimated levels of demand at the new price, and the probabilities of them occurring, are:

Selling price of $45

| Demand | Probability |
|---|---|
| 100,000 units | 0.45 |
| 120,000 units | 0.55 |

It is thought that at either of the higher sales and production levels, the variable cost per unit, and the probability of it occurring, will be as follows:

| Variable cost (per unit) | Probability |
|---|---|
| $20 | 0.40 |
| $18 | 0.60 |

---

203 The  probability that lowering the selling price to $45 per unit would increase profit is _____% (round to the nearest whole %)

204 The expected value of the company profit if the selling price is reduced to $45 per unit is $_____

205 On investigating the labour efficiency variance an organisation has found that there is typically a favourable variance of mean of $60,000 and a standard deviation of $5,000.

**The probability that the variance is less than $45,000 is _____% (answer to two decimal places)**

**The following data relate to Questions 206 and 207.**

A company expects to sell 1,000 units per month of a new product but there is uncertainty as to both the unit selling price and the unit variable cost of the product. The following estimates of selling price, variable costs and their related probabilities have been made:

| Selling price | | Unit variable cost | |
|---|---|---|---|
| $ per unit | Probability | $ per unit | Probability |
| 20 | 25% | 8 | 20% |
| 25 | 40% | 10 | 50% |
| 30 | 35% | 12 | 30% |

There are specific fixed costs of $5,000 per month expected for the new product.

**206** **The expected value of monthly contribution is:**

A    $5,890

B    $10,300

C    $10,890

D    $15,300

**207** **The probability of monthly contribution from this new product exceeding $13,500 is:**

A    24.5%

B    30.5%

C    63.0%

D    92.5%

**The following data relate to Questions 208 and 209.**

The committee of a new golf club is setting the annual membership fee. The number of members depends on the membership fee charged and economic conditions. The forecast annual cash inflows from membership fees are shown below.

| Membership fee | Membership level | | |
|---|---|---|---|
| | Low | Average | High |
| | $000 | $000 | $000 |
| $600 | 360 | 480 | 540 |
| $800 | 400 | 440 | 480 |
| $900 | 360 | 405 | 495 |
| $1,000 | 320 | 380 | 420 |

**208** **If the maximin criterion is applied the fee set by the committee would be:**

A    $600

B    $800

C    $900

D    $1,000

**209** If the minimax regret criterion is applied the fee set by the committee would be:

A     $600

B     $800

C     $900

D     $1,000

**210** Sarah owns a cafe and is trying to decide how many cakes she should bake each day. The demand is uncertain and Sarah has to make the cakes at the start of each day before the demand level is known.

The payoff table below shows the daily contribution Sarah can expect depending on the number of cakes baked and the level of demand that occurs.

| Level of demand | Number of cakes baked | | |
|---|---|---|---|
| | 20 | 25 | 30 |
| Low | $14 | $11.5 | $9 |
| Medium | $14 | $17.5 | $15 |
| High | $14 | $17.5 | $21 |

**The number of cakes Sarah should bake if she applies the maximax decision criterion is**

──────

**211** Sarah owns a cafe and is trying to decide how many cakes she should bake each day. The demand is uncertain and Sarah has to make the cakes at the start of each day before the demand level is known.

The payoff table below shows the daily contribution Sarah can expect depending on the number of cakes baked and the level of demand that occurs.

| Level of demand | Number of cakes baked | | |
|---|---|---|---|
| | 20 | 25 | 30 |
| Low | $14 | $11.5 | $9 |
| Medium | $14 | $17.5 | $15 |
| High | $14 | $17.5 | $21 |

**The number of cakes Sarah should bake if she applies the maximin decision criterion is**

──────

**212** Perfect information is described as:

A     100% accurate

B     85% accurate

C     Sometimes accurate

D     Never accurate

**213** A company is trying to decide which of four products it should launch. The demand is uncertain and is based on optimistic, likely and pessimistic forecasts. A regret matrix has been prepared showing the regret for each of the outcomes depending on the decision made.

| Regret matrix | Product | | | |
|---|---|---|---|---|
| Demand forecast | W | X | Y | Z |
| Optimistic | $43,000 | $0 | $73,000 | $38,000 |
| Likely | $15,000 | $5,000 | $35,000 | $0 |
| Pessimistic | $0 | $17,000 | $42,000 | $25,000 |

**If the company applies the minimax regret criterion to make decisions, which product would be chosen?**

A    W

B    X

C    Y

D    Z

**214** A company is considering launching one of two new products. If the product is successful in its first month there will be an opportunity to either make a further investment or to licence all future development to another company. The decision for the company is illustrated by the following decision tree:

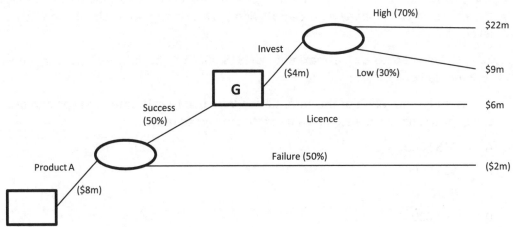

The profit outcomes do not include the cost of any investments made.

**What is the expected value at point G?**

A    $6m

B    $14.1m

C    $18.1m

D    $20.1m

**215** A toy retailer is considering introducing a new product and has to decide if the sales price should be $100, $105, $110 or $115. There is a 30% chance that demand could be high, a 50% chance that demand will be at a medium level and a 20% chance that demand will be low.

A payoff table below shows the profits based upon the sales price and the level of demand.

| Demand | Sales price | | | |
|---|---|---|---|---|
| | $100 | $105 | $110 | $115 |
| High | $1,700,000 | $1,725,000 | $1,700,000 | $1,625,000 |
| Medium | $700,000 | $600,000 | $450,000 | $250,000 |
| Low | $100,000 | $60,000 | $0 | $(80,000) |

The retailer has decided, using an expected value approach, the sales price should be set at $105 as this gives the highest expected profit of $880,000.

A market research company has since approach the retailer, it believes it can provide perfect information on the demand level.

**The maximum amount that should be paid for the information from the market research company is $_____ (Answer should be given to the nearest whole $)**

**216** Yum, a chocolate manufacturer, has to decide which of three new chocolate bars to launch. Demand is uncertain and could occur at one of three levels: low, medium or high. The management accountant uses expected values to make this type of decision and this has resulted in predicted expected profit of $142,000.

The market is highly competitive and so Yum has decided to employ the services of a market research company who can provide perfect information about the likely demand level.

Yum is prepared to pay a maximum of $15,000 for the information from the market research company.

**To determine the value of this information Yum had to calculate the expected profit with the information, what was the value of that expected profit?**

A    $157,000

B    $127,000

C    $112,000

D    $97,000

**217** A national chain of coffee shops has three potential new sites available:

| | | SHOP SIZE | | |
| --- | --- | --- | --- | --- |
| Demand | Probability | Small | Medium | Large |
| Strong | 0.2 | 354,600 | 894,300 | 1,413,200 |
| Good | 0.4 | 172,100 | 529,300 | 865,700 |
| Weak | 0.4 | 80,850 | 255,550 | 226,950 |

If the management team used an expected value approach they would have decided to open a large shop as this give the highest expected value of $719,700.

A market research company believes it can provide perfect information on the potential demand level.

**The maximum amount that should be paid for the information from the market research company is $_____ (Answer should be given to the nearest whole $)**

**218** A company is considering launching one of two new products. If the product is successful in its first month there will be an opportunity to either make a further investment or to outsource all future development to another company. The decision for the company is illustrated by the following decision tree:

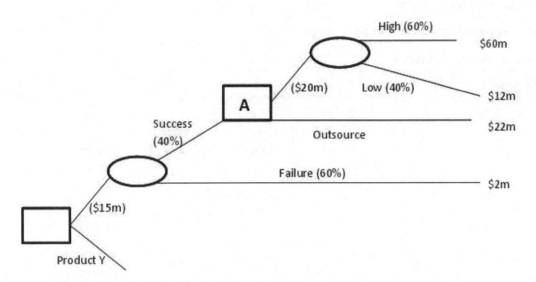

Profit outcome

The profit outcomes do not include the cost of any investments made.

**The expected value at point A on the decision trees (to the nearest $0.1m) is $_____m**

**219** A theatre has a seating capacity of 500 people and is considering engaging MS and her orchestra for a concert for one night only. The fee that would be charged by MS would be $10,000. If the theatre engages MS, then this sum is payable regardless of the size of the theatre audience.

The size of the audience for this event is uncertain, but based on past experience it is expected to be as follows:

|  | *Probability* |
|---|---|
| 300 people | 50% |
| 400 people | 30% |
| 500 people | 20% |

There is also some uncertainty regarding the contribution made from the sale of each theatre ticket. It is thought that there is a 70% chance that this would be $25 per person and a 30% chance that it would be $40 per person.

**Using expected values, the financial benefit from engaging MS for the concert is $_____**

**220** **Which of the following are disadvantages of using an expected value technique?**

|  | Disadvantage of EVs? |
|---|---|
| **Expected values only provides the most likely result** |  |
| **It ignores attitudes to risk** |  |
| **Only two possible outcomes can be considered** |  |
| **Probabilities are subjective** |  |
| **The answer provided may not exist** |  |

# Section 2

# ANSWERS TO OBJECTIVE TEST QUESTIONS

## COSTING TECHNIQUES

**1    B**

|  | $ |
|---|---:|
| Marginal costing profit | 45,000 |
| Less: fixed cost included in opening inventory (28,000 – 16,000) | (12,000) |
| Plus: fixed cost included in closing inventory (36,400 – 20,800) | 15,600 |
| Absorption costing profit | 48,600 |

**Alternative approach**

|  |  |
|---|---:|
| Increase in inventory using marginal costing | $4,800 |
| Increase in inventory using absorption costing | $8,400 |
| Difference = fixed overhead absorbed in inventory | $3,600 |

Inventory is increasing so absorption costing profit is higher than marginal costing profit by the amount of fixed overhead absorbed.

Absorption costing profit = $45,000 + $3,600 = $48,600

**2    B**

The opening inventory was 400 units and the closing inventory was 900 units, therefore inventory has increased.

If production is greater than sales then absorption costing will show the higher profit.

Difference in profit:    = Change in inventory × Fixed production cost per unit

= (900 – 400) × $29,500/5,000 units = $2,950

**3    A**

OAR = $330,000/220,000 = $1.50 per unit

|  | $ |
|---|---|
| Overhead absorbed (200,000 units × $1.50) | 300,000 |
| Actual overhead | 260,000 |
| Over absorbed | 40,000 |

**4    C**

| Return per minute | = | $\dfrac{\text{Selling price} - \text{material cost}}{\text{Time on bottleneck resource}}$ | |
|---|---|---|---|
| | = | $\dfrac{50 - 16}{8}$ | |
| | = | €4.25 | |
| Return per hour | = | €4.25 × 60 | = €255 |

**5**    Process **Y** is the bottleneck process.

| *Product S* | *Product T* |
|---|---|

Throughput of process X per day

$13.5 \text{ hrs} \times \dfrac{60}{5} = 162.00$          $13.5 \text{ hrs} \times \dfrac{60}{7.5} = 108.00$

(Production time: 15 − 1.5 = 13.5 hours)

Throughput of process Y per day

$14 \text{ hrs} \times \dfrac{60}{18} = 46.67$          $14 \text{ hrs} \times \dfrac{60}{12} = 70.00$

(Production time: 15 − 1 = 14 hours)

Process Y is the bottleneck process because it limits the production of both products to figures that are less than sales demand.

**6    A**

This is the CIMA *Official Terminology* definition of a bottleneck. With a throughput accounting approach, the aim should be to reduce or remove bottlenecks, so as to increase throughput.

**7    The throughput accounting ratio for this product is 0.778.**

Return per factory hour = $\dfrac{\$12 - \$5}{0.75 \text{ hrs}}$ = $9.333

Cost per factory hour = $144,000/12,000 = $12

TA ratio = 9.3333/12 = 0.778

**8    B**

The inventory will be valued at production cost, to be more precise at variable production cost.

Cost per unit = $\dfrac{\$40,000+\$12,600+\$9,400}{2,000\,\text{units}}$ = $31 per unit

No. of units in closing inventory = 2,000 – 1,750 = 250 units.

Therefore value of closing inventory = 250 units × $31 = $7,750.

**9    The value of inventory of X at 31 August using a throughput accounting approach is $5,000.**

Under throughput accounting, finished goods will be valued at direct material cost.

Cost per unit = $\dfrac{\$40,000}{2,000\,\text{units}}$ = $20 per unit

No. of units in closing inventory = 2,000 – 1,750 = 250 units.

Therefore value of closing inventory = 250 units × $20 = $5,000

**10    D**

Using throughput accounting inventory is valued at material cost

Inventory value = 20,000/4,000 × 400 units = $2,000

**11    The profit for the period using absorption costing is $7,170**

Value of closing inventory =$(13,500 + 11,800 + 32,400) × 200/2,000 = $5,770

|  | $ | $ |
|---|---|---|
| Sales (1,800 × $45) |  | 81,000 |
| Cost of production | 57,700 |  |
| Less closing inventory | 5,770 |  |
|  |  |  |
| Cost of sales |  | 51,930 |
|  |  |  |
| Gross profit |  | 29,070 |
| Non-production overhead |  | 21,900 |
|  |  |  |
| Profit |  | 7,170 |

**12    D**

Statements A, B and C are incorrect. JIT makes an organisation more vulnerable to disruptions in the supply chain, because there are no buffer inventories as protection against a breakdown in supply. JIT is easier to implement when an organisation operates within a narrow geographical area, and close to its suppliers. With little or no inventories, the risk of inventory obsolescence should not exist. Statement D is correct. When demand is difficult to predict, it becomes more difficult to operate a demand-driven operation.

**13**

| | Z1 | Z2 |
|---|---|---|
| | $ | $ |
| Selling price | 50 | 65 |
| Variable cost | 26.80 | 30.40 |
| | ——— | ——— |
| Contribution | 23.20 | 34.60 |
| No. of bottleneck min per unit | 12 | 16 |
| | | |
| Contribution per min | 1.93 | 2.16 |
| Priority | 2nd | 1st |

The optimum plan is to concentrate on Z2. We will make the maximum, which is 30 units (from Question 31).

Contribution = 30 units × $34.60 per unit = $1,038.

**14**

| | Z1 | Z2 |
|---|---|---|
| | $ | $ |
| Selling price | 50 | 65 |
| Direct material | 10 | 15 |
| | ——— | ——— |
| Throughput | 40 | 50 |
| No. of bottleneck min per unit | 12 | 16 |
| | | |
| Throughput per min | 3.33 | 3.13 |
| Priority | 1st | 2nd |

The optimum plan is to concentrate on Z1. We will make the maximum, which is 40 units.

Throughput = 40 units × $40 per unit = $1,600.

**15    D**

| | | Correct? |
|---|---|---|
| (i) | A cost driver is any factor that causes a change in the cost of an activity. | ✓ |
| (ii) | For long-term variable overhead costs, the cost driver will be the volume of activity. | ✓ |
| (iii) | Traditional absorption costing tends to under-allocate overhead costs to low-volume products. | ✓ |

Statement (i) provides a definition of a cost driver. Cost drivers for long-term variable overhead costs will be the volume of a particular activity to which the cost driver relates, so Statement (ii) is correct. Statement (iii) is also correct. In traditional absorption costing, standard high-volume products receive a higher amount of overhead costs than with ABC. ABC allows for the unusually high costs of support activities for low-volume products (such as relatively higher set-up costs, order processing costs and so on).

**16**

|  | | Facility-sustaining | Product-sustaining |
|---|---|:---:|:---:|
| (i) | General staff administration | ✓ | |
| (ii) | Plant management | ✓ | |
| (iii) | Technical support for individual products and services | | ✓ |
| (iv) | Updating of product specification database | | ✓ |
| (v) | Property management | ✓ | |

**17    A**

$$\text{Cost driver rate} = \frac{\text{Budgeted cost of orders}}{\text{Budgeted number of orders}} = \frac{\$110,010}{2,895} = \$38 \text{ for each order}$$

|  | $ |
|---|---|
| Cost recovered: 210 orders × $38 | 7,980 |
| Actual costs incurred | 7,650 |
| | ——— |
| Over-recovery of costs for four-week period | 330 |
| | ——— |

**18    The cost per unit attributed to product r for machine set ups is $0.52**

**Machine set up costs for Product R**

Budgeted machine set-ups:

| | | |
|---|---|---|
| Product D (1,000 × 3) | = | 3,000 |
| Product R (2,000 × 4) | = | 8,000 |
| Product P (2,000 × 6) | = | 12,000 |
| | | ——— |
| | | 23,000 |
| | | ——— |

$$\text{Cost per set up} = \frac{\$150,000}{23,000} = \$6.52$$

$$\text{Budgeted unit cost of R:} = \frac{\$6.52 \times 4}{50} = \mathbf{\$0.52}$$

**19    The total cost attributed to product Y for component deliveries using the proposed activity based costing system is $1,800**

| Cost driver | Number of cost drivers | Charge out rate |
|---|---|---|
| Number of component deliveries | 500 + 600 + 800 = 1,900 | $6,840/1,900 = $3.60 per delivery |

Charge to Product Y = 500 × $3.6 = $1,800

**20** **The profit for the period using marginal costing is $3,930.**

Value of closing inventory = $(13,500 + 11,800) × 200/2,000 = $2,530

|  | $ | $ |
|---|---|---|
| Sales | | 81,000 |
| Variable cost of production | 25,300 | |
| Less closing inventory | 2,530 | |
| | ——— | |
| Cost of sales | | 22,770 |
| | | ——— |
| Contribution | | 58,230 |
| Fixed overhead | | 54,300 |
| | | ——— |
| Profit | | 3,930 |
| | | ——— |

**21** **A**

|  | $ |
|---|---|
| Actual overhead incurred | 481,250 |
| Less under-absorbed overhead | 19,250 |
| | ——— |
| Overhead absorbed | 462,000 |
| | ——— |

Overhead absorbed = Actual standard hours charged × OAR

So OAR = overhead absorbed/actual standard hours charged = $462,000/38,500 = $12

OAR = Budgeted overheads/budgeted labour hours

So budgeted overheads = OAR × budgeted labour hours = $12 × 38,000 = $456,000

**22** **D**

Training should prevent future failure costs. Reworking costs are an internal failure cost.

**23** **B**

OAR = $500,000/2,000 = $250 per unit

Inventory has fallen by 300 units in the period.

Absorption costing profit will be 300 × $250 = $75,000 lower than marginal costing profit as some fixed overhead from previous periods will be brought forward to be matched against sales in the period using absorption costing. In marginal costing only the fixed overhead incurred in the period will be included in the profit statement.

**24** **C**

Option A may lead to over-absorption but this will depend on the extent to which actual overhead costs differ from budget. Option B describes under-absorption. Option D refers to budgeted overheads, which are used to calculate the OAR but otherwise not used in the calculation of under-/over-absorption.

**25** **The profit for the period using throughput accounting is $2,750.**

Value of closing inventory = $13,500 × 200/2,000 = $1,350

|  | $ | $ |
|---|---|---|
| Sales |  | 81,000 |
| Material costs | 13,500 |  |
| Less closing inventory | 1,350 |  |
| Cost of sales |  | 12,150 |
| Throughput |  | 68,850 |
| Operating expenses |  | 66,100 |
| Net profit |  | 2,750 |

**26** **The return per hour for product b is $780.**

|  | A $ | B $ | C $ |
|---|---|---|---|
| Selling price | 200 | 150 | 150 |
| Direct materials | 41 | 20 | 30 |
| Throughput | 159 | 130 | 120 |
| Machine P – minutes per unit | 12 | 10 | 7 |
| Return per factory minute | 159/12 | 130/10 | 120/7 |
|  | 13.25 | 13 | 17.14 |
| Return per factory hour × 60 minutes | $795 | $780 | $1,028 |

**27**

| Cost |
|---|
| Staff training |
| Units rejected before delivery |
| Returns of faulty units |
| Finished goods inspection |

| Classification |
|---|
| Prevention cost |
| Internal failure cost |
| External failure cost |
| Appraisal cost |

**28    A**

|  | $000 | $000 |
|---|---|---|
| Sales revenue |  | 820 |
| Variable cost of sales |  |  |
|    Variable production costs | 300 |  |
|    Less: closing inventory | 45 | 255 |
| Variable selling costs |  | 105 |
| Contribution |  | 460 |
| Fixed costs |  |  |
|    Production | 180 |  |
|    Selling | 110 | 290 |
| Profit |  | 170 |

**Working**

The closing inventory is valued at cost. As it is a marginal costing system the inventory is valued at variable cost, i.e. $300,000/1,000 units = $300 per unit. The closing inventory is 150 units, therefore the closing inventory value is $300/unit × 150 units = $45,000.

**29    The under-/over-absorption of fixed production overheads for the assembly department is $480.**

|  | Assembly | Finishing | Stores | Maintenance | Total |
|---|---|---|---|---|---|
| Budgeted overhead | 100,000 | 150,000 | 50,000 | 40,000 | 340,000 |
| Reapportion maintenance | 16,000 | 18,000 | 6,000 | (40,000) | – |
|  |  |  | 56,000 |  |  |
| Reapportion stores | 33,600 | 22,400 | (56,000) |  | – |
| Total overhead | 149,600 | 190,400 |  |  | 340,000 |

OAR for assembly department = $149,600/100,000 = $1.496 per unit

|  | $ |
|---|---|
| Overhead absorbed  120,000 × 1.496 | 179,520 |
| Overhead incurred | 180,000 |
| Under-absorption | 480 |

**30** **The cost per unit attributed to product I for processing time is $0.16**

Budgeted processing minutes:

| | | | |
|---|---|---|---|
| Product L (300,000 × 4) | = | 1,200,000 | |
| Product M (300,000 × 6) | = | 1,800,000 | |
| Product N (150,000 × 6) | = | 900,000 | |
| | | 3,900,000 | minutes |

Cost per minute = $\dfrac{\$156,000}{3,900,000}$ = $0.04

Budgeted unit cost of L = $0.04 × 4 = **$0.16**

**31** **A**

**32** **A**

| Cost | Prevention cost? |
|---|:---:|
| Inspection of raw materials | |
| Routine repairs and maintenance of machinery | ✓ |
| Returns of faulty products | |
| Machine breakdown repairs | |
| Training costs of operational staff | ✓ |

Prevention costs are those incurred in order to prevent poor quality.

Inspection of raw materials is an appraisal cost.

Returns from customers are an external failure cost.

Machine breakdown repairs are internal failure costs.

**33**

| Cost | True? |
|---|:---:|
| Conformance costs include prevention costs and appraisal costs | ✓ |
| As a company invests in preventing errors, costs of conformance will increase, and costs of non-conformance with fall | ✓ |
| Internal failure costs are costs of conformance | |
| External failure costs arise before the product is shipped to the customer | |
| Hiring quality control staff to inspect products is an example of a prevention cost | |

Internal failure costs are costs of non-conformance.

External failure costs arise after the goods have been sent to the customer.

Inspection staff are an example of appraisal costs.

**34    A**

Quality inspector salary is an appraisal cost, training costs are prevention costs, and collection from customers is an external failure cost

Items damaged in storage and fixing goods prior to delivery are both examples of internal failure costs as they have been discovered prior to delivery to the customer.

Incorrect answers are from adding together different combinations of the above figures.

**35    D**

Demand = 15,000 units, however 17% are rejected, therefore 15,000 = 83% of total units delivered to customers.

Total number of units despatched to customers is therefore 15,000/0.83 = 18,072.

This means that 3,072 units have to be replaced. Variable costs are $60 per unit and delivery is $5 therefore cost to replace is $65 per unit.

Total cost to replace of $65 × 3,072 units = $199,680

If you got answer (a) you used contribution of $20 per unit rather than variable cost of $60

Answer (b) was calculating the number of units to replace as 17% of 15,000.

Answer (c) ignores the transport cost of $5 per unit.

**36    The total gross profit for the deluxe speedboat using absorption costing is $16,800.**

Fixed production overheads = $69,600,000

Budgeted machine hours = (1,000 × 100) + (1,200 × 200) + (800 × 300) = 580,000

Fixed production overhead absorption rate = $69,600,000/580,000 = $120 per machine hour

|                        | Deluxe |
|------------------------|-------:|
|                        | $000   |
| Sales                  | 86,400 |
| Direct material        | 27,400 |
| Direct labour          | 13,400 |
| Production overhead     | 28,800 |
|                        | ────── |
| Gross profit           | 16,800 |
|                        | ────── |

**37    The total cost attributed to product c for quality inspections using an activity based costing system is $8,484**

| Cost driver | Number of cost drivers | Charge out rate |
|-------------|------------------------|-----------------|
| Number of quality inspections | (200 × 10) + (300 × 20) + (400 × 30) = 20,000 | $14,140/20,000 = $0.707 per inspection |

Charge to Product C = 400 × 300 × $0.707 = $8,484

**38    Advantages of an activity based costing system**

| Cost | Advantage? |
|---|:---:|
| Better cost control is possible | ✓ |
| Arbitrary allocations of costs are avoided | |
| Better product pricing is possible | ✓ |
| The choice of cost drivers is easy | |
| Can be applied to service companies | ✓ |

ABC provides better information on costs and how they are driven. It should therefore facilitate better cost control it can be difficult to attach cost drivers to activities and this can make the system expensive to set up initially. It will also still involve some arbitrary cost allocations. For example, in a service industry it may be difficult to determine what drives the chief executive's salary and to determine how this should be allocated to services.

Despite these faults, ABC should still provide a *better* allocation of costs to products when compared to traditional costing methods and this should then result in better pricing decisions. The success of ABC in manufacturing industries has led to the adoption of the technique in service industries – and exam questions are just as likely to involve service industries as they are to involve a manufacturing company.

# VARIANCE ANALYSIS

**39    C**

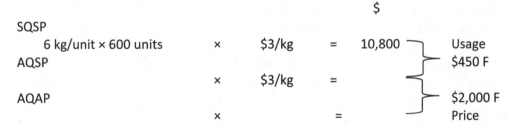

```
                                                          $
SQSP
      6 kg/unit × 600 units        ×      $3/kg    =   10,800 ⌉   Usage
AQSP                                                          ⌐── $450 F
                                   ×      $3/kg    =          ⌡
AQAP                                                          ⌐── $2,000 F
                                   ×               =          ⌡   Price
```

This is a 'backwards' question. Given some information including the variances, we then have to work backwards to find some missing numbers – here, the number of kg purchased.

```
                                                          $
SQSP
      6 kg/unit × 600 units        ×      $3/kg    =   10,800 ⌉   Usage
AQSP                                                          ⌐── $450 F
      3,450 kg^{Bal 2}              ×      $3/kg    =   10,350^{Bal 1} ⌡
AQAP                                                          ⌐── $2,000 F
                                   ×               =          ⌡   Price
```

The question can also be answered as follows:

| | Kg | |
|---|---:|---|
| 600 units should use (× 6 kg) | 3,600 | |
| Usage variance in kg ($450(F)/3) | 150 | (F) |
| Therefore 600 units did use | 3,450 | |

Given no change in stock levels, usage quantity = purchase quantity.

**40    C**

Option A is an ideal standard, option B is an attainable standard and option D is a current standard.

**41    D**

**Direct labour variance**

|  |  |  |  |  | $ |  |
|---|---|---|---|---|---|---|
| AHSR |  |  |  |  |  |  |
|  | 24,000 hrs | × | $15/hr | = | 360,000 | ⎤ |
| AHAR |  |  |  |  |  | $24,000 F |
|  |  |  |  | = | 336,000 | ⎦ Rate |

**42    A**

**Variable overhead variance**

|  |  |  |  |  | $ |  |
|---|---|---|---|---|---|---|
| SHSR |  |  |  |  |  |  |
|  | 2 hrs/unit × 11,000 units | × | $6/hr | = | 132,000 | ⎤ Efficiency |
| AHSR |  |  |  |  |  | $12,000 A |
|  | 24,000 hrs | × | $6/hr | = | 144,000 | ⎦ |

**43    D**

|  | $ |
|---|---|
| Budget overhead | 2,500,000 |
| Actual overhead | 2,010,000 |
| Expenditure variance | 490,000 F |

**44    C**

OAR = $2,500,000/500,000 = $5 per unit

|  |  |
|---|---|
| Budgeted volume | 500,000 units |
| Actual volume | 440,000 units |
|  | 60,000 units |
| × OAR per unit | × $5 |
| Volume variance | $300,000 A |

**45    A**

|  | $ |
|---|---|
| Expected cost = ($800 + $0.0002 × 4,100$^2$) × 1.03 | 4,287 |
| Actual cost | 5,000 |
|  | 713A |

**46    B**

Inventories are valued at standard prices, so the material price variance must be calculated by reference to the quantity purchased.

**Material variances**

$

SQSP

     6 kg/unit × 2,192 units    ×    $6.75/kg  =  88,776

AQSP                                        Usage

     13,050 kg           ×    $6.75/kg  =  88,087.50    $688.50 F

For a usage variance the quantity must be the quantity used (13,050 kgs).

$

AQSP

     12,550 kg           ×    $6.75/kg  =  84,712.50

AQAP                                    $11,812.50 F

                                =    72,900    Price

For a price variance the quantity must be the quantity purchased (13,050 kgs – reduction in inventory = 13,050 – 500 = 12,550 kgs).

Alternatively:

|  | $ |  |
|---|---|---|
| 12,550 kgs should cost ($6.75/kg) | 84,712.50 |  |
| They did cost | 72,900.00 |  |
| Price variance | $11,812.50 | (F) |

| Usage variance | kgs |  |
|---|---|---|
| 2,192 finished units should use (× 6) | 13,152 |  |
| They did use | 13,050 |  |
| Usage variance in kgs | 102 kgs | (F) |

Usage variance in $ = 102 kgs (F) × $6.75/kg (standard price) = $688.50 (F)

**47    C**

This is the CIMA definition.

**48     C**

**Labour variances**

$

SHSR
    10 hrs/unit × 6,200 units     ×     $9.50/hr     =     589,000 ⎤ Efficiency
AHSR                                                                        ⎱ $8,455 A
          62,890 hrs          ×     $9.50/hr     =     597,455 ⎰
AHAR                                                                        ⎱ $1,043 F
                                                        =     596,412 ⎱ Rate

The variances could also be calculated as follows:

| Rate variance: | $ |
|---|---|
| 62,890 hours should cost (× $9.50) | 597,455 |
| They did cost | 596,412 |
| | ——— |
| Labour rate variance | 1,043     (F) |
| | ——— |

| Efficiency variance: | *Hours* |
|---|---|
| 6,200 units should take (× 10) | 62,000 |
| They did take | 62,890 |
| | ——— |
| Efficiency variance in hours | 890     (A) |
| | ——— |

Efficiency variance in $ = 890 hours (A) × $9.50 per hour = $8,455 Adverse.

**49     The adverse fixed overhead volume variance is $10,000.**

$$\text{Absorption rate} = \frac{\$170,000}{42,500} = \$4/\text{unit}$$

| | *Units* |
|---|---|
| Budgeted output | 42,500 |
| Actual output | 40,000 |
| | ——— |
| Volume variance in units | 2,500     (A) |
| Standard fixed overhead cost/unit | × $4 |
| | ——— |
| Fixed overhead volume variance in $ | $10,000     (A) |
| | ——— |

**50** **The favourable fixed overhead efficiency variance is $24,000.**

|  |  | Hours |  |
|---|---|---|---|
| Standard hours for actual production | (104,040/20,400) × 20,000 | 102,000 | |
| Less Actual hours | | 100,000 | |
| | | | |
| Volume variance in units | | 2,000 | (F) |
| Standard fixed overhead cost/hour | ($1,248,480/104,040) | × $12 | |
| | | | |
| Fixed overhead efficiency variance in $ | | $24,000 | (F) |

**51** **B**

| Actual hours | | 660 | |
|---|---|---|---|
| Less Budgeted hours | 2 × 320 ops | 640 | |
| | | | |
| Capacity variance in hours | | 20 | (F) |
| Standard fixed overhead cost/hour | ($108,000/[320 × 2 hours]) | × $168.75 | |
| | | | |
| Fixed overhead capacity variance in $ | | $3,375 | (F) |

**52** **D**

| Standard hours for actual production | 2 hours × 300 ops | 600 | |
|---|---|---|---|
| Less Actual hours | | 660 | |
| | | | |
| Efficiency variance in hours | | 60 | (A) |
| Standard fixed overhead cost/hour | ($108,000/[320 × 2 hours]) | × $168.75 | |
| | | | |
| Fixed overhead efficiency variance in $ | | $10,125 | (A) |

**53    B**

### Labour variance

|  |  |  |  | $ |  |
|---|---|---|---|---|---|
| SHSR |  |  |  |  |  |
| 0.75 hrs/unit × 11,000 units  × |  | $20/hr | = | 165,000 | Efficiency |
| AHSR |  |  |  |  | $5,000 F |
| 8,000 hrs |  × | $20/hr | = | 160,000 |  |

The variances could be calculated as follows:

|  | Hours |  |
|---|---|---|
| 11,000 units should take (× 0.75 hr) |  |  |
|  | 8,250 |  |
| did take | 8,000 |  |
|  |  |  |
| Efficiency variance in hours | 250 | Favourable |
| Standard rate per hour | × $20 |  |
|  |  |  |
| Efficiency variance in $ | $5,000 | Favourable |

**54    C**

### Variable overhead variance

|  |  |  |  | $ |  |
|---|---|---|---|---|---|
| AHSR |  |  |  |  |  |
| 8,000 hrs |  × | $15/hr | = | 120,000 |  |
| AHAR |  |  |  |  | $12,000 A |
|  |  |  | = | 132,000 | Expenditure |

The variance could also be calculated as follows:

|  | $ |  |
|---|---|---|
| 8,000 hours should cost × $15) | 120,000 |  |
| did cost | 132,000 |  |
|  |  |  |
| Expenditure variance | 12,000 | Adverse |

**55    D**

### Sales price variance

|  | $ |  |
|---|---|---|
| Std selling price | 500 |  |
| Actual selling price | 465 |  |
|  |  |  |
| Sales price variance | 35 | (A) |
| × Actual no of units sold | × 642 |  |
|  |  |  |
|  | 22,470 |  |

**56    C**

**Sales volume contribution variance**

|  | Units |  |
|---|---|---|
| Budgeted quantity sold | 600 |  |
| Actual quantity sold | 642 |  |
| Sales volume variance in units | 42 | (F) |
| × Std contribution per unit (25% × $500) | × $125 |  |
|  | $5,250 | (F) |

**57    The favourable material mix variance for product E using the average valuation method was $85**

Standard input of E is $\dfrac{3.50}{4.0+3.5+2.5 \text{ litres}}$ = 35% x 10,000 litres = 3,500 litres

Actual input of E was = 3,600 litres

The mix variance (in litres) = 3,600 – 3,500 = 100 litres

Weighted average standard price per litre = $\dfrac{\$58.50}{4.0+3.5+2.5\,\text{litres}}$ = $5.85 per litre

The materials mix variance = Variance in litres × Difference in price (weighted av. standard price – Ind. Material std price)

= 100 litres x ($5.85 - $5)

= $85

**58    A**

The operational labour efficiency variance uses the revised standard time of 12 minutes.

SHSR

$\$$

$^{12}\!/_{60}$ × 370 × $10/hr =    740

AHSR

80 hrs ×    $10/hr =    800

Efficiency $60 A

**59    B**

Standard cost per litre of output = $\dfrac{\$58.50}{9\,\text{litres}}$ = $6.50/litre

The standard yield = 90% x 10,000 litres = 9,000 litres

The actual yield = 9,100 litres

Yield variance in litres = 9,100 – 9,000 = 100 litres Favourable

Total yield variance = 100 litres x $6.50/lire = $650 Favourable

## 60 A

The fixed overhead volume variance is the difference between budgeted and actual production volume multiplied by the standard absorption rate per unit. This is the same as the difference between budgeted value of fixed overheads (budgeted volume × standard absorption rate per unit) and standard fixed overheads absorbed by actual production (actual volume × standard absorption rate per unit).

## 61 The total favourable material mix variance for October 20X3 was $49.2.

| | Actual mix Litres | Standard mix Litres | Difference Litres | | Price $ | Variance $ | |
|---|---|---|---|---|---|---|---|
| X | 984 | 885.6 | 98.4 | (A) | 2.50 | 246.0 | (A) |
| Y | 1,230 | 1,328.4 | 98.4 | (F) | 3.00 | 295.2 | (F) |
| Totals | 2,214 | 2,214.0 | nil | | | 49.2 | (F) |

## 62 The total adverse material mix variance for October 20X3 was $151.2.

Expected output $= \dfrac{2,214}{30} = 73.8$ units

Actual output $= 72.0$ units

Shortfall $= 1.8$ units

1.8 units × $84/unit $= $151.2$ (A)

An alternative would be only 73 complete units of output were expected, thus the shortfall would be 1 unit. The variance would be 1.0 × $84 per unit = $84 adverse.

## 63

| | | Correct? |
|---|---|---|
| (i) | The standard allowance for material wastage was set too high. | |
| (ii) | Material purchased was of a lower quality than standard. | ✓ |
| (iii) | Lower grade and less experienced employees were used than standard. | ✓ |
| (iv) | More material was purchased than budgeted for the period because output was higher than budgeted. | |

Event (i) is more likely to result in a favourable usage variance therefore it is not correct. Event (ii) could cause an adverse usage variance since a lower quality material might lead to higher wastage and a higher level of quality control rejects. Event (iii) could cause an adverse usage variance because lower skilled employees might waste material and quality control rejects might again be higher. Event (iv) would not necessarily cause an adverse usage variance. The usage variance is based on the expected usage for the actual output, not on the budgeted usage for the budgeted output.

**64**   **The actual level of production for the period was 360,000 units**

OAR = $1,500,000/300,000 = $5 per unit

Fixed production overhead variance is the level of over/under absorption. An adverse variance means that overhead is under absorbed.

|                              | $         |
| ---------------------------- | --------- |
| Overhead absorbed            |           |
| Actual output × $5           | ?         |
| Actual overhead              | 1,950,000 |
|                              | ───────   |
| Under absorbed               | 150,000   |

**65**   **B**

Less experienced employees are likely to take longer than standard to produce a given level of output. The result would be an adverse variable overhead efficiency variance. Option A is more likely to result in a favourable variable overhead efficiency variance because employees are likely to work faster than standard. Option C might also result in a favourable efficiency variance because higher quality material is likely to be easier to process, thus saving time against standard. Option D would result in an adverse variable overhead expenditure variance but would not directly affect the variable overhead efficiency variance.

**66**   **Using the average valuation basis, the adverse material mix variance for material C was $8.**

|            | Actual usage Litres |        | Standard mix Litres | Mix variance Litres |     | Rate $        | Mix variance $ |     |
| ---------- | ------------------- | ------ | ------------------- | ------------------- | --- | ------------- | -------------- | --- |
| Material C | 200                 | (6/10) | 180                 | 20                  | (A) | (3 – 2.60)    | 8              | (A) |
| Material D | 75                  | (3/10) | 90                  | 15                  |     | (1 – 2.60)    | 24             |     |
|            |                     |        |                     |                     | (F) |               |                | (A) |
| Material E | 25                  | (1/10) | 30                  | 5                   | (F) | (5 – 2.60)    | 12             | (F) |
|            | ───                 |        | ───                 | ───                 |     |               | ───            |     |
|            | 300                 |        | 300                 | Nil                 |     |               | 20             | (A) |
|            | ───                 |        | ───                 | ───                 |     |               | ───            |     |

**67**   **Using the average valuation basis, the adverse material yield variance was $52.**

|                                          | Litres   |     |
| ---------------------------------------- | -------- | --- |
| Standard usage for actual output of X2   | 280      |     |
| Actual usage                             | 300      |     |
|                                          | ───      |     |
| Yield variance in litres                 | 20       | (A) |
| × weighted average standard price per litre | × $2.60 |     |
|                                          | ───      |     |
| Yield variance in $                      | $52      | (A) |
|                                          | ───      |     |

**68**   **The favourable sales volume profit variance for the period was $20,000.**

**Sales volume profit variance**

| | |
|---|---|
| Budgeted sales volume (units) | 100,000 |
| Actual sales volume (units) | 110,000 |
| | 10,000   favourable |
| Standard profit per unit ($10 – $8) | $2 |
| | $20,000   Favourable |

**69**   **D**

Working 100 hours more than the standard time to produce the actual output would result in an adverse labour efficiency and fixed overhead efficiency variances.  If the standard hours are 100 more than the original budget then it would result in a favourable fixed overhead volume variance.

**70**   **B**

**Mix variance**

| Liquid | Standard mix | Actual mix | Mix variance | Standard price | Mix variance |
|---|---|---|---|---|---|
| | ltr | | | $ | $ |
| X | 2,250 | 2,200 | 50 F | 16 | 800 F |
| Y | 2,700 | 2,750 | 50 A | 25 | 1,250 A |
| | 4,950 l | 4,950 l | | | 450 A |

**71**   **D**

| | Actual mix (kg) | Actual quantity/ Standard mix (kg) | Difference (kg) | Standard price ($) | Mix variance ($) |
|---|---|---|---|---|---|
| P | 1,030 | 1,000 | 30A | 75 | 2,250 A |
| Q | 560 | 600 | 40F | 100 | 4,000 F |
| R | 410 | 400 | 10A | 125 | 1,250 A |
| | 2,000 | 2,000 | | | 500 F |

**72**   **C**

| | |
|---|---|
| 2,000 kgs should produce 2,000/100 × 90 | 1,800 kg of output |
| did produce | 1,910 kg of output |
| Difference | 110 F |
| Value at standard cost per kg ($9,250/90) | $11,306 F |

**73    B**

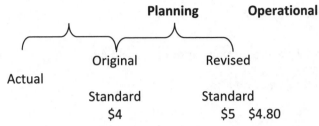

Planning price variance = ($4 − $5) × 3 kg × 10,000 units = $30,000 A

**74    D (SEE NEXT ANSWER)**

**75    B**

Material variance

|  |  |  |  | $ |  |
|---|---|---|---|---|---|
| SQSP | | | | | |
| | 3 kg/unit × 10,000 units × | $5/kg | = | 150,000 | Usage |
| AQSP | | | | | $10,000 A |
| | 32,000 kg × | $5/kg | = | 160,000 | |
| AQAP | | | | | $6,400 F |
| | 32,000 kg × | $4.80/kg | = | 153,600 | Price |

The standards here are the revised standards.

**76    The idle time variance for April was $49,500.**

Idle hours = 61,500 − 56,000 = 5,500

Standard rate per hour = $540,000/60,000 = $9

Idle time variance = 5,500 × $9 = $49,500 Adverse

**77    The favourable labour efficiency variance for April was $23,400.**

| 14,650 units should take | 60,000/15,000 = 4 hours per unit | 58,600 hours |
|---|---|---|
| Did take | | 56,000 hours |
| | | |
| Difference | | 2,600 hours F |
| Value at standard rate per hour ($9) | | $23,400 F |

**78    B**

8,200 × ($31 − $26) = $41,000 F

**79    A**

OAR = $34,800/8,700 = $4 per unit

Standard profit per unit = $26 − $10 − $4 = $12

Volume variance = (8,700 − 8,200) × $12 = $6,000 A

**80    A**

(8,700 – 8,200) × $4 = $2,000 A

**81    The adverse material price planning variance was $4,480.**

Material price planning variance

| | |
|---|---|
| Original standard price | $4.10 |
| Revised standard price | $4.50 |

.40 A × 11,200 units = $4,480 A

**82    The adverse operational material usage variance was $3,600.**

Operational material usage variance

| | |
|---|---|
| 1,600 units should use (× 7) | 11,200 kg |
| did use | 12,000 kg |

800 kg A

Valued at revised standard price ($4.50)                $3,600 A

**83**

| | |
|---|---|
| 11,500 units should use 5 hours each | 57,500 hours |
| Did use | ? |
| Variance in hours | |
| Value at $12 per hour | |
| Labour efficiency variance | $30,000 A |

*Working backwards:*

The variance in hours = $30,000/12 = 2,500 A

The actual hours used are 57,500 + 2,500 = 60,000

| | |
|---|---|
| 60,000 hours should cost (× $12) | 720,000 |
| Did cost | ? |
| Labour rate variance | 45,000 A |

*Working backwards:*

The actual labour cost = $765,000

So the actual rate paid per hour = $765,000/60,000 = $12.75.

**84** **The total favourable sales mix profit variance for the period using the individual units method is $50.**

| Product | Standard mix | Actual mix | Variance (units) | Standard profit/unit | Sales mix variance |
|---|---|---|---|---|---|
| A | 725 | 750 | 25 (F) | $5.00 | $125.00 (F) |
| B | 725 | 700 | 25 (A) | $3.00 | $75.00 (A) |
| Total | 1,450 | 1,450 | | | $50.00 (F) |

Where the standard mix is the total actual sales units (1,450) divided by the total budgeted sales units (1,600) and multiplied by the budgeted units of each individual product (800 for A)

**85**

| Variance | Cause |
|---|---|
| Material price variance | Increase in costs charged by a supplier |
| Material usage variance | Increased wastage due to a machine malfunction |
| Labour rate variance | Unexpected pay award |
| Labour efficiency variance | Improved operating procedures for staff |

An increase in costs from a supplier would cause an adverse material price variance. Increased wastage would cause an adverse material usage variance but might not affect labour efficiency. An unexpected pay award would give an adverse labour rate variance, and improved operating procedures would make the staff more efficient and as such a favourable efficiency variance.

**86** **The total adverse sales mix profit variance for the period using the individual units method is $600.**

Standard weighted average profit per unit

| Product | Sales budget (units) | Standard profit/unit | Total profit |
|---|---|---|---|
| A | 800 | $5.00 | $4,000 |
| B | 800 | $3.00 | $2,400 |
| Total | 1,600 | | $6,400 |

Sales quantity profit variance

| | |
|---|---|
| Budgeted sales units | 1,600 |
| Actual sales units | 1,450 |
| | 150 (A) |
| Average profit per unit | $4 |
| Sales quantity profit variance | $600 (A) |

Average profit per unit = $6,400/1,600 units = $4.00 per unit

**87**   The total favourable sales mix profit variance for the period using the individual units method is $620.

| Product | Standard mix | Actual mix | Variance (units) | Standard profit/unit | Sales mix variance |
|---|---|---|---|---|---|
| A | 3,450 | 4,000 | 550 (F) | $2.00 | $1,100 (F) |
| B | 9,200 | 7,500 | 1,700 (A) | $1.50 | $2,550 (A) |
| C | 10,350 | 11,500 | 1,150 (F) | $1.80 | $2,070 (F) |
| Total | 23,000 | 23,000 | | | $62.00 (F) |

**88**   The total favourable sales quantity profit variance for the period using the individual units method is $5,130.

Standard weighted average profit per unit

| Product | Sales budget (units) | Standard profit/unit | Total profit |
|---|---|---|---|
| A | 3,000 | $2.00 | $6,000 |
| B | 8,000 | $1.50 | $12,000 |
| C | 9,000 | $1.80 | $16,200 |
| Total | 20,000 | | $34,200 |

Average profit per unit = $34,200/20,000 units = $1.71 per unit

*Sales quantity profit variance*

| | |
|---|---|
| Budgeted sales units | 20,000 |
| Actual sales units | 23,000 |
| | 3,000   (F) |
| Average profit per unit | $1.71 |
| Sales quantity profit variance | $5,130   (F) |

**89**

| | Caused by purchasing better quality? |
|---|---|
| Favourable fixed overhead expenditure variance | |
| Favourable material usage variance | ✓ |
| Adverse labour rate variance | |
| Favourable labour efficiency variance | ✓ |
| Favourable labour rate variance | |

**90**   **A**

It is usual for the production manager to finalise the production schedule so if the labour has been less efficient than expected then this would be his responsibility.

**91** **The favourable sales mix variance for Product B is $26,250.**

|  | Actual sales @standard mix (units) | Actual sales @ actual mix (units) | Variance (units) | Standard profit $ | Variance $ |
|---|---|---|---|---|---|
| Product B | 2,475 | 3,000 | 525 F | 50.00 | 26,250 F |
| Product C | 2,025 | 1,500 | 525 A | 53.75 | 28,219 A |
|  | 4,500 | 4,500 |  |  | 1,969 A |

**92** **B**

It is usual for the purchasing department to negotiate prices with suppliers. So if a supplier is charging more than the standard price this would fall under the responsibility of the purchasing manager.

Better quality materials should result in less wastage of material which in turn will allow the employees to produce more units in the time allowed as fewer units will be scrapped or require rework.

**93** **The expenditure variance for the set ups was $100.**

Standard price (SP) = 6,820/220 = 31

Flexed standard cost = AQ × SP = 200 × $31 = 6,200

Actual cost = 6,300

Variance = 6,200 – 6,300 = $100A

**94**

|  | Affected? |
|---|---|
| Sales price variance |  |
| Sales quantity profit variance | ✓ |
| Direct labour rate variance |  |
| Fixed overhead expenditure variance |  |
| Fixed overhead capacity variance | ✓ |

The difference in between marginal and absorption costing is in the treatment of fixed overheads. This will impact on the profit per unit which will impact on the sales quantity profit variance. In marginal costing there is no fixed overhead volume variance and therefore there would be no fixed overhead capacity variance.

**95** **B**

Standard quantity (SQ) = 75 supervisors/5,000 employees × 5,500 employees = 82.5 supervisors

Standard price (SP) = $7,500/75 supervisors = $100 per supervisor

Standard cost (SQ × SP) = 82.5 × $100 = $8,250

Actual cost = $8,085

Total variance = 8,250 – 8,085 = $165 Favourable

**96** **The adverse variable overhead efficiency variance is $6,230**

Number of hours per unit for Product X = $14/$7 = 2 hours

Number of hours per unit for Product Y = $10.50/$7 = 1.5 hours

Variable overhead cost per hour = $3/2 hours (or $2.25/1.5 hours) = $1.50 per hour

Variable overhead efficiency variance =

((12,000 × 2 hrs) + (16,000 × 1.5 hrs)) − 46,000) × $1.50 per hour = $3,000 Adverse

**97** **C**

Total budgeted profit = ($4 x 4,000) + ($3 x 6,000) = $34,000

Weighted average profit per unit = $34,000/10,000 = $3.40

|  | Actual sales @standard mix (units) | Budget sales @ standard mix (units) | Variance (units) | Standard profit $ | Variance $ |
|---|---|---|---|---|---|
| Product R | 4,800 | 4,000 | 800 F | 3.40 | 2,720 F |
| Product S | 7,200 | 6,000 | 1,200 F | 3.40 | 4,080 F |
|  | 12,000 | 10,000 |  |  | 6,800 F |

# DECISION MAKING

**98** **B**

The material is in regular use by the organisation and so would be replaced if it is used on the special order. The material is readily available at a price of $3.24 per kg.

Therefore the relevant cost of the material is 1,250 kgs × $3.24 = $4,050.

**99** **B**

$$\text{Breakeven sales revenue} = \frac{\text{fixed costs}}{\text{C/S ratio}}$$

$$800,000 = \frac{\$320,000}{\text{C/S ratio}}$$

$$\text{C/S ratio} = \frac{\$320,000}{\$800,000} = 40\%$$

Sales revenue required to achieve a target profit of $50,000

$$= \frac{\$320,000 + 50,000}{40\%} = \$925,000$$

**100  D**

| | |
|---|---:|
| Replacement material cost saved (4 kg @ $5.00) | 20.00 |
| Less further processing cost ($0.75 × 5 kg) | 3.75 |
| | |
| Value of M in current use, for each unit made | $16.25 |

Therefore opportunity cost of using M on the job being tendered for =

$16.25/5 kg = $3.25 per kg.

**101  B**

The book value is an historic cost and therefore not relevant. There is no intention to replace material X. There are two options for material X, scrap at a value of 50p per kg or use as a replacement for material Y, which would save $4 per kg ($6 – $2). The latter is the preferable option so the relevant cost is $4 per kg for 10 kgs = $40.

**102  C**

Labour is in short supply so there is an opportunity cost. The contribution from Contract Z will still be earned but will be delayed. The relevant cost is therefore the wages earned plus the penalty fee.

($15 × 100) + ($1,000) = $2,500

**103  A**

It is cheaper to hire the external consultant for $4,500 rather than pay the $5,000 bonus to the existing junior consultant. The consultant's salary is not a relevant cost as the consultant will still be paid even if the project does not proceed.

**104  The expected relevant cost of Material XY for use when evaluating the viability of the contract is $12,900**

If contract is carried out and stock is needed, relevant cost is the replacement value of $15,000. Probability = 0.6

If contract is carried out and stock is not needed, relevant cost is the sales value of $12,000. Probability = 0.4

Whatever happens, $900 holding cost is incurred. This will be saved if the contract is carried out.

Expected value = $15,000 × 0.6 + $12,000 × 0.4 – $900 = $12,900.

**105 A**

3,700 kg × $3.80 + 500 kg × $6.30 = $17,210

### Tutorial note

*The company needs 4,200 kg. It has 3,700 kg in stock. It will therefore need to buy 500 kg and these can be bought for $6.30 per kg.*

*The tricky bit is the value to the company of the 3,700 kg in stock. The $4.50 original purchase price is of course a sunk cost and cannot be relevant.*

*The stock can be sold for $3.20 per kg, so this is its very minimum value. The stock is worth $3.20 per kg unless the company has an even better alternative.*

*Well, there is a better alternative. The company can take the stock and, by spending $3.70 per kg on it, can turn it into something worth $7.50 per kg. If something will be worth $7.50 if we spend $3.70 on it, then it is at present worth $3.80. This then is the value of the stock to the company and to fulfil the contract the company will use 3,700 kg of stock with a value of $3.80 per kg.*

**106 The cost per unit of product Y is $74**

By-product revenue = 3,000 × $0.20 = $600.

Therefore costs of the process = $45,000 − $600 = $44,400.

| | | | $ |
|---|---|---|---|
| Sales revenue, product X | = 250 × $80 = | | 20,000 |
| Sales revenue, product Y | = 400 × $100 = | | 40,000 |
| | | | ——— |
| Total joint product sales revenue = | | | 60,000 |
| | | | ——— |

Joint costs are apportioned:

To X: $44,400 × 20/60 = $14,800

To Y: $44,400 × 40/60 = $29,600.

Cost per unit of product Y = $29,600/400 = $74.

**107 C**

Weighted average contribution to sales ratio:

$$\frac{(35\% \times 6) + (20\% \times 5) + (30\% \times 4)}{(6 + 5 + 4)}$$

$$= \frac{(210 + 100 + 120)\%}{15}$$

= 28.667%

Target contribution is obtained by adding back fixed costs to the target profit figure:

$40,000 + $160,000 = $200,000.

Therefore the sales required: 200,000/0.28667 = $697,666 i.e. $698,000 to the nearest $1,000.

**108  B**

If the margin of safety budgeted in period 3 is 21.015%, then the breakeven number of units in the period is:

6,570 – (6,570 × 21.015%) = 5,189 units

At this level, contribution is equal to the level of fixed costs.

Contribution at this volume is:

5,189 × 35% × $72 = $130,763.

So fixed costs are $130,763 (which is nearest to B, i.e. $131,000).

**109  The relevant cost of the 2,000 kgs of material J to be included in the quotation is $16,000**

Since material J is in regular use and is readily available in the market, its relevant cost is the replacement price of $8/kg.

So 2,000 kgs × $8/kg = $16,000

**110**

|  | Required? |
|---|:---:|
| The product-specific fixed costs | ✓ |
| The product mix ratio | ✓ |
| General fixed costs | ✓ |
| The method of apportionment of general fixed costs | |
| Individual product gross contribution to sales ratios | ✓ |

To calculate breakeven, we need total fixed costs (product-specific plus general fixed costs), the C/S ratio for each product and the product sales mix. The method of apportioning fixed costs is irrelevant.

**111  A**

First calculate the contribution to sales ratio for U:

| S | 60% | × | $\frac{1}{3}$ | = | 20.00% | |
|---|---|---|---|---|---|---|
| T | 45% | × | $\frac{1}{3}$ | = | 15.00% | |
| U | 51% | × | $\frac{1}{3}$ | = | 17.00% | (balancing figure) |
| Total | | | | = | 52.00% | |

By changing the mix, the overall ratio becomes:

| S | 60% | × | 45% | = | 27.00% |
|---|---|---|---|---|---|
| T | 45% | × | 20% | = | 9.00% |
| U | 51% | × | 35% | = | 17.85% |
| Total | | | | = | 53.85% |

## 112  C

The minimum sales values must be satisfied first, earning a contribution of (30% × 400) + (20% × 400) + (25% × 400) = $300,000. This leaves 850 – 300 = $550,000 contribution still to be earned before breakeven.

We want to produce the products in the order E, G, F, since this will earn the maximum contribution from the least sales.

Producing the maximum sales of E will generate further contribution of $(1,200 – 400) × 30% = $240,000. Thus there is still 550 – 240 = $310,000 still to be earned.

$310,000 contribution from G requires sales of $\dfrac{310}{0.25}$ = $1,240,000.

The minimum breakeven sales value is therefore:

| | |
|---|---:|
| E (maximum) | 1,200 |
| F (minimum) | 400 |
| G (minimum + 1,240) | 1,640 |
| | 3,240 |

## 113  The margin of safety is 25.6%

Weighted average C/S ratio equals:

$$\frac{(3\times 32\%)+(5\times 48\%)}{3+5} = 42\%$$

Breakeven point = $\dfrac{\text{Fixed costs}}{\text{C/S ratio}}$ = $\dfrac{\$200,000}{0.42}$ = 476,190

Margin of safety = $640,000 – $476,190 = $163,810 or 25.6%

## 114  A

| Volume | Contribution per contract | Total contribution | Selling price | Total revenue |
|:---:|:---:|:---:|:---:|:---:|
| | $ | $ | $ | $ |
| 2 | 550 | 1,100 | 1,000 | 2,000 |
| 3 | 500 | 1,500 | 750 | 2,250 |
| 5 | 220 | 1,100 | 400 | 2,000 |
| | | 3,700 | | 6,250 |

Average C/S ratio = $\dfrac{\$3,700}{\$6,250}$ = 0.592

Breakeven point = $\dfrac{\$1,000,000}{0.592}$ = $1,689,189

## 115  D

| | |
|---|---|
| Contribution per unit $14 – $6 | $8 |
| Breakeven point (BEP) = $24,400 ÷ $8 | 3,050 units |
| With new method: | |
| Contribution per unit $15 – $5 | $10 |
| BEP = $31,720 ÷ $10 | 3,172 units |

BEP increases by 122 units

## 116  A

Let x be level of activity.  At point of indifference both profits are the same.

| | | |
|---|---|---|
| 8x – 24,400 | = | 10x – 31,720 |
| 31,720 – 24,400 | = | 10x – 8x |
| x | = | 3,660 |

## 117  The monthly breakeven sales revenue is $594,000

A weighted average contribution to sales (C/S) ratio needs to be calculated:

$$\frac{(3\times40\%) + (7\times30\%) + (5\times35\%)}{3+7+5} = 33.67\%$$

The monthly breakeven sales value is therefore the monthly fixed costs divided by the weighted average C/S ratio:

$200,000/0.3367 = $594,000

## 118  The minimum contribution that must be earned by a unit of product Y to make it worth producing units of product Y in a profit-maximising budget is $4

Product Y uses more materials per unit than product X. If product X is manufactured, it will earn a contribution of $6 per kilogram consumed and $4 per labour hour. To make product Y worth making, it must earn at least the lower amount of $6 per kilogram ($24 per unit) or $4 per labour hour ($4 per unit). So the answer is $4.

You could possibly work this out by drawing a linear programming graph: if the contribution per unit of Y exceeds $24, the company will make Y only. If the contribution per unit of Y is less than $4, it will make X only. If the contribution per unit of Y is over $4 but less than $24, the optimal production mix will be a combination of X and Y.

## 119 A

| Product cost per unit | | E1 | | E2 | | E3 | | E4 |
|---|---|---|---|---|---|---|---|---|
| | | $ | | $ | | $ | | $ |
| Conversion costs | | 40 | | 65 | | 65 | | 55 |
| Less general fixed costs | 0.5 × | | 0.5 × | | 0.6 × | | 0.6 × | |
| absorbed | $30 | 15 | $30 | 15 | $30 | 18 | $30 | 18 |
| | | — | | — | | — | | — |
| Variable conversion cost | | 25 | | 50 | | 47 | | 37 |
| Material cost | | 24 | | 33 | | 41 | | 30 |
| | | — | | — | | — | | — |
| Total variable cost | | 49 | | 83 | | 88 | | 67 |
| Selling price | | 90 | | 112 | | 123 | | 103 |
| | | — | | — | | — | | — |
| Contribution | | 41 | | 29 | | 35 | | 36 |
| | | — | | — | | — | | — |
| Contribution for each $1 | | 1.7 | | 0.8 | | 0.8 | | 1.2 |
| spent on material | | 1 | | 8 | | 5 | | 0 |
| Ranking | | 1st | | 3rd | | 4th | | 2nd |

## 120 C

A shadow price for a scarce resource is its opportunity cost. It is the amount of contribution that would be lost if one unit less of that resource were available. It is similarly the amount of additional contribution that would be earned if one unit more of that resource were available. (This is on the assumption that the scarce resource is available at its normal variable cost.)

## 121 D

$$\$10.50 + \frac{\$10}{2}$$

## 122 D

The company maximises contribution by producing Qutwo. Contribution per unit of material is:

$$\frac{\$8.50}{2.5\,\text{kg}} = \$3.40 \text{ and this is the shadow price.}$$

## 123 D

| | R | S | T |
|---|---|---|---|
| | $ | $ | $ |
| Contribution per unit | | | |
| $(100 − 15 − 20 − 15) | 50 | | |
| $(150 − 30 − 35 −20) | | 65 | |
| $(160 − 25 − 30 − 22) | | | 83 |
| Direct labour cost per unit | 20 | 35 | 30 |
| Contribution per $1 of direct labour | 2.50 | 1.85 | 2.77 |
| Profitability ranking | 2nd | 3rd | 1st |

**124** **The minimum total cost at which BJS Company can obtain the full requirement of components is $563,000**

Calculate extra cost per hour if buy externally.

|  | P | Q | R |
|---|---|---|---|
|  | $ | $ | $ |
| Internal cost | 45 | 70 | 56 |
| External cost | 65 | 78 | 80 |
| Extra cost | 20 | 8 | 24 |
| Hours per unit | 9 | 5 | 12 |
| Extra cost per hour | $2.22 | $1.60 | $2.00 |

To minimise cost make P internally, then R and finally Q.

|  | Units | Total hours | Cost per unit | Total cost |
|---|---|---|---|---|
| P – internal | 3,000 | 27,000 | $45 | $135,000 |
| R – internal | 1,916 | 23,000 | $56 | $107,296 |
| R – external | 1,084 |  | $80 | $86,720 |
| Q – external | 3,000 |  | $78 | $234,000 |
| **Total** |  | **50,000** |  | **$563,016** |

**125** **The cost-plus selling price of one unit of product L should be $100**

Total annual costs = $60 x 50,000 units = $3,000,000

Required annual return = $10,00,000 × 20% = $2,000,000

Return as a percentage of total cost =2,000,000/3,000,000 = 67%

Required cost-plus selling price = $60 + (67% + $60) = $100

**126** **D**

|  | $/unit |
|---|---|
| Direct materials | 9.00 |
| Direct labour | 14.00 |
| Total direct cost | 23.00 |
| Production overhead absorbed (2 hours x $4.50 per hour) | 9.00 |
| Total production cost | 32.00 |
| Mark-up for non-production costs (10% x $32) | 3.20 |
| Full cost | 35.20 |
| Profit mark-up (20/80 x 35.20) | 8.80 |
| Target selling price | 44.00 |

**127  C**

If S1 is unlimited then the products must be ranked on the basis of their contribution per machine hour:

|  |  | Ranking |
|---|---|---|
| X1 | $12/6 = $2.00 | 2nd |
| X2 | $5/4 = $1.25 | 3rd |
| X3 | $8/3 = $2.66 | 1st |

|  |  | Hours required |
|---|---|---|
| Minimum X2 | 100 × 4 | 400 |
| Produce X3 | 200 × 3 | 600 = a total of 1,000 hours used 7,000 hours remaining |
| Produce X1 | $\dfrac{7,000}{6}$ | = 1,166 |

**128  The percentage increase in the unit variable cost that would result in Product X breaking even at the budgeted level of activity is 30%**

Contribution per unit is $10 × 60% = $6.  Hence variable cost is $4.

Breakeven point is $120,000 ÷ $6 = 20,000 units.

With a safety margin of 20% the budget was 25,000 units.

Keeping all variables fixed, except the variable cost per unit, we can now find the new variable cost per unit.

Let $x be the variable cost per unit.

If the company is to breakeven at 25,000 units then:

| Contribution | = | Fixed costs |  |
|---|---|---|---|
| ($10 – x).25,000 units | = | 120,000 |  |
| x |  | = | 5.20 |

The new variable cost is $5.20 per unit.

This is $1.20 higher than the original cost, i.e. 30% higher.

**129  The maximum price that a profit-maximising company should be willing to pay to the outside supplier for the components is $40,000**

If components are purchased outside:

|  | $ |
|---|---|
| Contribution earned elsewhere | 25,000 |
| Variable cost saving | 15,000 |
|  | ——— |
| Maximum price to pay | 40,000 |
|  | ——— |

**130**

|  | Meal? |
|---|---|
| *Most profitable* | L |
| *Least profitable* | K |

|  | K | L | M |
|---|---|---|---|
| Sales price | $5.00 | $3.00 | $4.40 |
| Less variable costs | $3.60 | $1.80 | $2.15 |
| Contribution per meal | $1.40 | $1.20 | $1.25 |
| Minutes | ÷ 10 | ÷ 4 | ÷ 8 |
| Contribution per minute | $0.14 | $0.30 | $0.16 |

**131**

|  | Limitation? |
|---|---|
| Linear relationships must exist | ✓ |
| There can only be two products | ✓ |
| There can only be two scarce resources |  |
| All variables must be completely divisible | ✓ |
| A computer must be used to find the optimal point |  |

Linear programming can cope with any number of constraints and the solution does not always need to be solved by a computer.

**132  D**

When making a further processing decision it is necessary to consider incremental revenues and incremental costs. Apportionment of joint costs is NOT relevant to the decision.

**133**

|  | Shadow price >0? |
|---|---|
| Direct labour hours | ✓ |
| Material A |  |
| Material B |  |
| Machine hours |  |

Only resources that meet at the optimal point will have a shadow price. This is at point B, where the direct labour line meets line R. The other constraints lines are above this point and there therefore must be surplus of these resources available. Resources that have a surplus do not have a shadow price.

### 134 B

This should be based on contribution per unit:

| Product | J | L |
|---|---|---|
| | $/unit | $/unit |
| Selling price | 115 | 120 |
| Direct material A ($10 per kg) | 20 | 10 |
| Direct material B ($6 per kg) | 12 | 24 |
| Skilled labour ($14 per hour) | 28 | 21 |
| Variable overhead ($4 per machine hour) | 14 | 18 |
| Contribution | 41 | 47 |

And the iso-contribution line is 41J + 47L = M

### 135 The maximum amount of Material A available is 2,000 kgs

The line crosses the horizontal axis at coordinates T = 0 and R = 1,000. If each unit of R takes 2 kgs of Material A, then there must be 2,000 kgs of Material A available.

# BUDGETING

### 136

| | Purpose of budgeting? |
|---|---|
| Communication | ✓ |
| Authorisation | ✓ |
| Sales maximisation | |
| Co-ordination | ✓ |

The budget communicates to individual managers what is expected of them in the forthcoming budget period and how much expenditure they can incur in meeting their targets. Thus communication is a purpose of budgeting. An agreed budget provides authorisation for individual managers to incur expenditure in undertaking the activities in their own budget centre. Therefore authorisation is a purpose of budgeting. Although an organisation might have an objective of maximising sales and might set a budget to enable them to achieve this objective, the maximisation of sales is not in itself a purpose of budgeting. Therefore is not correct. Individual budget targets are set within the framework of the plan for the organisation as a whole and in this way a budget provides a means of coordinating the efforts of everyone within the organisation.

### 137 D

See workings in next answer.

## 138  D

In the year ended October 20X3 total variable costs were $850,000 × 60% = $510,000. These can be analysed as follows:

|  | People | Packages (kg) | Total |
|---|---|---|---|
| Variable costs 50:50 |  |  | $510,000 |
|  | $255,000 | $255,000 |  |
| Units in year | 4,420 | 30,500 | – |
| Cost per unit | $57.69 | $8.36 | – |
| Adjusted cost (× 1.02) | $58.84 | $8.53 | – |
| Activity for period to 31 January 20X4 | 1,150 | 8,100 | – |
| Total related costs | $67,666 | $69,093 | $136,759 |

## 139

|  | E | F | G | Total |
|---|---|---|---|---|
| Budgeted number of batches to be produced: | 75,000/200 | 120,000/60 | 60,000/30 |  |
|  | = 375 | = 2,000 | = 2,000 |  |
| Machine set-ups per batch: | 5 | 3 | 9 |  |
| Total machine set-ups | 1,875 | 6,000 | 18,000 | 25,875 |

So budgeted cost per set-up: $180,000/25,875 = $6.96 per set-up

Therefore the budgeted machine set-up cost per unit of F produced is:

($6.96 × 3)/60 = $0.35 per unit or $6.96 × 6,000/120,000 = $0.35 per unit

## 140  D

Production overhead:

|  | Units |  | $ |
|---|---|---|---|
| High | 800 | (× 1.75) | 1,400 |
| Low | 500 | (× 2.50) | 1,250 |
|  | 300 |  | 150 |

Variable cost = $150/300 = $0.50

Fixed cost = $1,400 – (800 × $0.50) = $1,000

Other overhead:

|  | Units |  | $ |
|---|---|---|---|
| High | 800 | (× 0.625) | 500 |
| Low | 500 | (× 1.00) | 500 |

This is a wholly fixed cost.

Variable cost per unit:

|  | $ |
|---|---|
| Direct material | 2.00 |
| Direct labour | 1.50 |
| Variable production overhead | 0.50 |
|  | 4.00 |

Period fixed cost:

|  | $ |
|---|---|
| Fixed production overhead | 1,000 |
| Other overhead | 500 |
|  | 1,500 |

## 141  C

Note that the material usage figure is not required.

|  | Units |
|---|---|
| Sales | 30,000 |
| Add closing inventory (3,500 × 1.35) | 4,725 |
| Less opening inventory | (3,500) |
| Production | 31,225 |

## 142  D

## 143  The expected level of production in May is 15,900 units

|  | April units | May units | June units |
|---|---|---|---|
| **Production budget** |  |  |  |
| Sales | 12,000 | 15,000 | 18,000 |
| Add closing inventory | 4,500 | 5,400 |  |
|  | 16,500 | 20,400 |  |
| Less opening inventory | 3,600 | 4,500 |  |
| Production | 12,900 | 15,900 |  |

**144 C**

At output of 6,000 units, overhead = 6,000 × $3.20 = $19,200

At output of 10,000 units, overhead = 10,000 × $3.00 = $30,000

$\therefore$ Variable overhead/unit = $\dfrac{\$30,000 - \$19,200}{10,000 - 6,000}$ = $2.70

Fixed overhead = $19,200 − (6,000 × $2.70) = $3,000

At activity of 7,350 units, budgeted production overhead = $3,000 + (7,350 × $2.70) = $22,845

**145 D**

| Quarter | Value of x | | Trend units | | | Forecast sales units |
|---|---|---|---|---|---|---|
| 1 | 25 | y = (26 × 25) + 8,850 | 9,500 | × 85% | = | 8,075.0 |
| 2 | 26 | y = (26 × 26) + 8,850 | 9,526 | × 95% | = | 9,049.7 |
| 3 | 27 | y = (26 × 27) + 8,850 | 9,552 | × 105% | = | 10,029.6 |
| 4 | 28 | y = (26 × 28) + 8,850 | 9,578 | × 115% | = | 11,014.7 |
| | | | | | | 38,169.0 |

Difference between Q1 and Q4 budgeted sales = 11,014.7 − 8,075.0 = 2,939.7 units

**146 B**

A zero based budgeting system begins each budget from scratch every time. All expenditure on the activity must be justified from zero and the method of carrying out each activity must be re-evaluated as if it were being carried out for the first time.

**147 The overhead cost for RP for month 240 is $39,000**

Orders = [100,000 + (30 × 240)] × 1.08 = 115,776

Overhead cost = $10,000 + ($0.25 × 115,776) = $38,944

Answer is $39,000

**148 D**

| Trend | = | 9.72 + (5.816 × 23) |
|---|---|---|
| | = | 143.488 |
| Seasonal factor | + | 6.5 |
| Forecast | | 149.988 |

To the nearest whole unit, the forecast number of units to be sold is 150.

**149  C**

| | | |
|---|---|---|
| Probability of rainy summer | = | $1.0 - 0.4 = 0.6$ |
| Expected value of sales volume | = | $(80,000 \times 0.4) + (120,000 \times 0.6)$ |
| | = | 104,000 units |

**150  The total fixed costs for a budgeted output of 36,000 units are $86,000**

It is known that there is a stepped fixed cost of $10,000 above 35,000 units. Removing the stepped fixed cost at 40,000 units leaves $184,000.

(i)  Variable cost per unit = $\dfrac{\$184,000 - \$143,500}{40,000 - 25,000} = \$2.70$

(ii)  At 25,000 units

| | |
|---|---|
| Total cost | 143,500 |
| Total variable cost  $2.70 \times 25,000$ | 67,500 |
| | ——— |
| Fixed cost | 76,000 |
| | ——— |

Therefore fixed cost at 36,000 units = $76,000 + $10,000 = $86,000

**151  C**

Budgetary slack is also called budget bias. Budget holders may sometimes try to obtain a budget that is easier to achieve. They may do this either by bidding for expenditure in excess of what they actually need or, in the case of sales budgets, by deliberately setting easy revenue targets.

**152  Assuming that the first quarter of year 1 is time period reference number 1, the forecast for sales units for the third quarter of year 7, is 300,750 units**

We have been given the trend equation.  We need to plug in the value for x so that we can find y.  X is the time period reference number and for the first quarter of year 1 is 1.  The time period reference number for the third quarter of year 7 is 27.  (Just keep adding 1 to the time period reference number for each new quarter, thus quarter 2, year 1, x = 2; quarter 3, year 1, x = 3; quarter 4, year 1, x = 4; quarter 1, year 2, x = 5, etc.)

$$y = 25,000 + 6,500 \times 27 = 200,500 \text{ units}$$

This is the trend we now need to multiply by the seasonal variation for quarter 3:

Forecast = 200,500 × 150/100 = 300,750 units.

**153  C**

| | Machine hours | $ |
|---|---|---|
| High | 12,212 | 39,477 |
| Low | 8,480 | 31,080 |
| | ——— | ——— |
| Change | 3,732 | 8,397 |
| | ——— | ——— |

| | | |
|---|---|---|
| Variable cost per machine hour | = | $8,397/3,732 |
| | = | $2.25 |
| Fixed cost = $39,477 − (12,212 × $2.25) | = | $12,000 |

Budget cost allowance for 9,340 machine hours:

|  |  | $ |
|---|---|---|
| Fixed cost |  | 12,000 |
| Variable cost (9,340 × $2.25) | = | 21,015 |
|  |  | 33,015 |

**154  The value for purchases of J to be included in the cash budget for February is $36,400**

|  | April<br>units | May<br>units |
|---|---|---|
| **Materials budget** |  |  |
| Production (units) | 4,300 | 5,300 |
| × No. of units of material per unit of product | × 1 unit | × 1 unit |
| Usage quantity (units) | 4,300 | 5,300 |
| Add closing inventory | 1,325 |  |
|  | 5,625 |  |
| Less op inventory | 1,075 |  |
| Purchase quantity (units) | 4,550 |  |
| × purchase price | × $8 |  |
| Purchase cost ($) | 36,400 |  |

The purchase cost of materials in January is $36,400.  This will be paid in February.

**155  C**

The P/V line will move down as profit will be lower at all units of sales. The gradient represents the C/S ratio and this will be unchanged.

**156  D**

This is the definition of a master budget.

**157  The budgeted cost per month for quality testing is $34,000**

The monthly variance = $\dfrac{\$102,000}{12\,\text{months}}$ = $8,500

The variance number of tests = $\dfrac{\$8,500}{\$850\,\text{per test}}$ = 10 tests

Budgeted tests must therefore have been = 50 − 10 = 40 per month.

Budgeted quality test costs per month = 40 tests x $850 per test = $34,000

**158    The entry for 'purchases' that will be shown in the cash budget for August is $76,000**

**September are $86,000**

**October are $106,000**

Purchases are sold at cost plus 25% so cost of sales is 100/125= 0.8 × Sales

Closing inventory = 0.5 × Following month's cost of sales

Closing inventory = Opening inventory of the following month

| Month | Sales | Cost of sales | Opening inventory | Closing inventory | Purchase | Paid |
|---|---|---|---|---|---|---|
| July | 100 | 80 | 40 | 36 | 76 | |
| August | 90 | 72 | 36 | 50 | 86 | **76** |

**159   C**

| High Low Method | Activity | $ | |
|---|---|---|---|
| | 6,500 | 33,000 | |
| | 4,500 | 29,000 | |
| Difference | 2,000 | 4,000 | |
| So the variable cost | = $4,000/2,000 | = $2 per unit | |
| Substitute into either activity | 6,500 | 33,000 | Total cost |
| | 6,500 × $2 | 13,000 | Variable cost |
| | Difference | $20,000 | Fixed cost |

The estimated production cost for 5,750 units = 5,750 × $2 + $20,000 = $31,500

**160    The revenue that needs to be generated by Product Z for S plc to achieve the budgeted profit is $16 million**

($10m × 0.15) + ($20m × 0.1) + ?m = $5.5m + $2m

$3.5m + ?m = $7.5m       so ? = $4m

Revenue needed to ensure a profit of $2m = 4/0.25 = $16m

**161    The total receipts expected in month 4 are $114,144**

| | Sales | $ |
|---|---|---|
| Cash receipts | $108,000 × 20% | 21,600 |
| Month 2 | $120,000 × 80% × 40% × 0.985 | 37,824 |
| Month 1 | $105,000 × 80% × 58% | 48,720 |
| B/f | | 6,000 |
| | | $114,144 |

**162    The budgeted profit per unit for Product X using activity-based budgeting is $48.40**

| Overhead cost per unit | X |
| --- | --- |
| | $ |
| Receiving/inspecting quality assurance (W1) | 504,000 |
| Production scheduling/machine set-up (W2) | 390,000 |
| Total overhead cost | 894,000 |
| Units produced and sold | 15,000 |
| Overhead cost per unit | 59.60 |

| **Activity based profit from Product X** | $ |
| --- | --- |
| Selling price | 183.00 |
| Direct material | 40.00 |
| Direct labour | 35.00 |
| Overhead cost per unit | 59.60 |
| | |
| Profit per unit | 48.40 |

**Workings**

(W1)   1,800/5,000 × 1,400,000 = 504,000

(W2)   260/800 × 1,200,000 = 390,000

**163    The  material purchases budget for the next year is $656,400**

| Budgeted sales | 24,000 | units |
| --- | --- | --- |
| Plus closing inventory | 2,000 | units |
| Less opening inventory | (500) | units |
| Budgeted production | 25,500 | units |

| Raw material required | 25,500 units × 2 kg | = 51,000 kg |
| --- | --- | --- |
| Plus closing inventory | 2,000 units × 2 kg | =  4,000 kg |
| Less opening inventory | | (300) kg |
| Raw material purchases | | 54,700 kg |
| | | |
| Raw material purchases budget | 54,700 kg × $12 | = $656,400 |

**164    The labour cost budget for the year is $2,112,000**

Labour hours for production

36,000 units × 4 hours = 144,000 hours

Idle time = 10% of total available hours, therefore total available hours need to be:

144,000 hours/0.9 = 160,000 hours

Labour cost budget ($)

160,000 hours × 20% = 32,000 hours × ($12 × 1.50) = $576,000

160,000 hours × 80% = 128,000 hours × $12 = $1,536,000

The total labour cost budget = 576,000 + 1,536,000 = $2,112,000

**165** **Using the additive model, after adjusting for seasonal variations, the expected sales of Product A for Quarter 3 of Year 2 is 30,000 units**

| Quarter | Trend sales units | Actual sales units | Variation units |
|---|---|---|---|
| 1 | 13,000 | 14,000 | +1,000 |
| 2 | 16,000 | 18,000 | +2,000 |
| 3 | 19,000 | 18,000 | −1,000 |
| 4 | 22,000 | 20,000 | −2,000 |

Year 2 Quarter 1 = 10,000 + (3,000 × 5) = 25,000 + 1,000 = 26,000 units

Year 2 Quarter 2 = 10,000 + (3,000 × 6) = 28,000 + 2,000 = 30,000 units

Year 2 Quarter 3 = 10,000 + (3,000 × 7) = 31,000 − 1,000 = 30,000 units

**166** **C**

| | $ |
|---|---|
| Cash received from previous period | 460,000 |
| Sales for this budget period | 5,400,000 |
| | 5,860,000 |
| Credit sales not paid until next period ($5,400,000 × 80% × 1/12) | (360,000) |
| Total cash received | 5,500,000 |

**167** **The budgeted trade payable days at the end of next year are 41 days**

Trade payables outstanding at end of this year = $474,500/365 × 45 = $58,500

Purchases budget for next year = $474,500 × 1.1 = $521,950

Trade payable days at end of next year = $58,500/$521,950 × 365 = 40.9 days

**168** **The material purchases budget for the forthcoming year is $560,000**

Production budget for Product D

| | Units | |
|---|---|---|
| Opening inventory | (6,000) | |
| Sales | 36,000 | |
| Closing inventory | 3,000 | i.e. 36,000/12 |
| Production | 33,000 | |

Purchases budget for raw material C

| | kg | |
|---|---|---|
| Opening inventory | (2,000) | |
| Production | 66,000 | i.e. 33,000 × 2 kg |
| Closing inventory | 6,000 | i.e. 3,000 × 2 kg |
| Purchases | 70,000 | |

The purchases budget for raw material C is therefore:

70,000 kg × $8 per kg = $560,000

**169   The answer is $4,933,500**

| Budgeted sales | 144,000 | units |
|---|---|---|
| Plus Closing inventory | 12,000 | units |
| Less Opening inventory | (6,500) | units |
| Budgeted production | 149,500 | units |

149,500 × 2 hours per unit = 299,000 hours

80% × 299,000 = 239,200 hours × $15 = $3,588,000

20% × 299,000 = 59,800 hours × $(15 × 1.5) = 1,345,500

Total labour cost budget = $4,933,500

**170   B**

Variable cost per unit

$$\frac{\text{Change in cost}}{\text{Change in units}} \quad \frac{113,000 - 55,000}{3,000 - 1,000} = \$29.00/\text{Unit}$$

Total fixed cost

| Total cost @ 3,000 units | 113,000 |
|---|---|
| Less variable cost (3,000 units × $29.00/unit) | 87,000 |
| Total fixed cost | $26,000 |

Flexed budget for 2,750 units

| Variable cost (2,750 units × $29.00/unit) | 79,750 |
|---|---|
| Fixed cost | 26,000 |
| Total cost | $105,750 |

**171  B**

| | |
|---|---|
| Variable cost per unit | = ($2,840,000 – $2,420,000)/(190,000 – 160,000) |
| | = $420,000/30,000 |
| | = $14 per unit |
| Fixed costs | = $2,840,000 – (190,000 × $14) |
| | = $180,000 |
| Total costs at 205,000 units | = (205,000 × $14) + $180,000 |
| | = $3,050,000 |

**172  C**

| | |
|---|---|
| Cost before stepped increase | = $2,840,000 – $30,000 = $2,810,000 |
| Variable cost per unit | = ($2,810,000 – $2,420,000)/(190,000 – 160,000) |
| | = $390,000/30,000 = $13 |
| Fixed costs at 190,000 units | = $2,840,000 – (190,000 × $13) |
| | = $370,000 |
| Total costs at 175,000 units | = (175,000 × $13) + ($370,000 – $30,000) |
| | = $2,615,000 |

**173  The total adverse profit variance for the period was $5,040**

| | Original budget | Flexed budget | Actual | Variances |
|---|---|---|---|---|
| Sales units | 1,000 | 1,380 | 1,380 | |
| Sales revenue | 100,000 | 138,000 | 133,860 | 4,140 (A) |
| Direct material | 40,000 | 55,200 | 57,800 | 2,600 (A) |
| Direct labour | 20,000 | 27,600 | 27,000 | 600 (F) |
| Variable overhead | 15,000 | 20,700 | 18,600 | 2,100 (F) |
| Fixed overhead | 10,000 | 10,000 | 11,000 | 1,000 (A) |
| | | | | |
| Profit | 15,000 | 24,500 | 19,460 | 5,040 (A) |

**174  A**

Year 2, quarter 3 is period 7

Trend sales  = 22,000 + 800 (7)
           = 27,600 units

Adjusted for seasonal variations = 27,600 × 1.30 = 35,880 units

**175  B**

| | |
|---|---|
| Trend sales for quarter 2 year 1 | = 22,000 × 800(2) |
| | = 23,600 units |
| Actual sales for quarter 2 year 1 | = 23,600 × 90% |
| | = 21,240 units |
| Seasonal variation using additive model | = 21,240 – 23,600 |
| | = –2,360 |

**176** **The entry for 'purchases' that will be shown in the cash budget for September is $86,000**

Purchases are sold at cost plus 25% so cost of sales is 100/125= 0.8 × Sales

Opening inventory = 0.5 × this month's cost of sales

Closing inventory = 0.5 × following month's cost of sales

Closing inventory = Opening inventory of the following month

| Month | Sales | Cost of sales | Opening inventory | Closing inventory | Purchase | Paid |
|---|---|---|---|---|---|---|
| August | 90 | 72 | 36 | 50 | 86 | |
| September | 125 | 100 | 50 | 56 | 106 | **86** |

**177** **C**

|  | $ |
|---|---|
| Cash paid from previous period | 540,000 |
| Purchases for this budget period | 6,800,000 |
| | 7,340,000 |
| Purchases not paid until next period | (425,000) |
| ($6,800,000 × 75% × 1/12) | |
| Total cash paid | 6,915,000 |

**178** **C**

The direct material and the royalty fee are both direct costs and therefore not included with in the overhead budget.

**179**

| Cost |
|---|
| Commission paid to an agent for selling the product |
| Electricity used in the factory |
| Depreciation of factory building |
| Packaging material to protect the product |

| Budget |
|---|
| Selling overhead budget |
| Variable production overhead budget |
| Fixed production overhead budget |
| Distribution overhead budget |

**180  C**

By use of the high/low method

Variable cost per unit

Change in cost

$\dfrac{24{,}000 - 18{,}000}{2{,}000 - 1{,}000}$ = $6/Unit

Change in units

Total fixed cost

| | |
|---|---:|
| Total cost @ 2,000 units | 24,000 |
| Less variable cost (2,000 units × $6/unit) | 12,000 |
| Total fixed cost | $12,000 |

Flexed budget for 1,980 units

| | |
|---|---:|
| Variable cost (1,980 units × $6/unit) | 11,880 |
| Fixed cost | 12,000 |
| Total cost | $23,880 |

**181  The budgeted fixed overheads in the period were $200,000**

As the overheads are absorbed on a labour hours basis the number of units and machine hours are irrelevant.  So the budget will be 16,000 hours * $12.50 per hour = $200,000

**182  C**

Total labour hours = (1,000 units * 0.5 hours) + (2,000 units * 2 hours) = 4,500 hours

Total machine hours = (1,000 units * 0.25 hours) + 2,000 units * 1.5 hours) = 3,250 hours

Total variable overheads = 3,250 hours * $1.50 per hour  = $4,875

Total fixed overheads = 4,500 hours * $1.95 per hour = $8,775

Total overheads = $4,875 + $8,775 = $13,650

**183  A**

The annual rent for the head office building is an administrative overhead not a production overhead, the electricity usage would be a variable production overhead rather than a fixed production overhead, and the materials is a direct cost rather than an overhead.

**184  D**

A is a fixed budget. B is a zero based budget. C is a flexed budget

**185**

|  | Not a criticism? |
|---|:---:|
| It may make managers, staff and unions feel threatened | ✓ |
| It encourages slack | |
| It is time consuming as it involves starting from scratch | ✓ |
| It encourages wasteful spending | |
| It includes past inefficiencies as costs are not scrutinised | |

ZBB may make staff feel threatened as they need to justify all costs and activities. This is less likely with incremental budgeting.

Incremental budgeting is not a slow process, as budgets are based on prior period figures.

**186 B**

|  | Original Budget | Flexed Budget |
|---|---:|---:|
| Sales units | 1,000 | 1,200 |
|  | $ | $ |
| Sales revenue | 100,000 | 120,000 |
| Direct material | 40,000 | 48,000 |
| Direct labour | 20,000 | 24,000 |
| Variable overhead | 15,000 | 18,000 |
| Fixed overhead | 10,000 | 10,000 |
| Profit | 15,000 | 20,000 |

**187**

|  | Characteristic of rolling budgets? |
|---|:---:|
| Budgets are more likely to be realistic as there is a shorter period between preparation and actual events occurring | |
| Updates to budgets are only made when they are foreseeable | ✓ |
| They reduce uncertainty in budgeting | |
| They force management to look ahead more frequently | |
| Each item of expenditure must be fully justified before inclusion in the budget | ✓ |

Rolling budgets are updated on as regular basis (for example, monthly or quarterly), not just when a change is foreseeable. The final point is a characteristic of zero based budgeting.

**188 D**

Zero based budgeting is the method in which all activities are re-evaluated.

A budget updated regularly is a rolling budget.

**189 D**

**190 The sales receipts for month 2 are budgeted to be $10,180**

| Month | 1 | 2 | 3 |
|---|---|---|---|
| Sales units | 1,500 | 1,750 | 2,000 |
| Sales (Units × $10) | 15,000 | 17,500 | 20,000 |
| Paid in month – 20% × 0.98 | 2,940 | 3,430 | 3,920 |
| 45% in the following month | | 6,750 | 7,875 |
| 25% in 3rd month | | | 3,750 |
| | | | |
| Receipts | 2,940 | 10,180 | 15,545 |

**191 D**

| Month | 1 | 2 | 3 |
|---|---|---|---|
| Production units | 1,850 | 1,800 | 2,020 |
| Rate per unit | $1.20 | $1.20 | $1.20 |
| | | | |
| Variable overhead cost | $2,220 | $2,160 | $2,424 |
| | | | |
| 60% in month | 1,332 | 1,296 | 1,454 |
| 40% in following month | | 888 | 864 |
| | | | |
| Payment | 1,332 | 2,184 | 2,318 |

**192 A**

Zero based budgeting starts each year from scratch.

**193**

| | Limitations of 'What if' analysis? |
|---|---|
| Only one variable changes at a time | ✓ |
| It assesses the risk to the closing cash balance | |
| It provides an assessment of how responsive the cash flows are to changes in variables. | |
| Probabilities of changes are not accounted for | ✓ |
| It directs attention to critical variables | |

The other options are advantages of using what if analysis.

# THE TREATMENT OF UNCERTAINTY IN DECISION MAKING

**194** If orders must be placed before the daily demand is known, the number of units that should be purchased at the beginning of each day in order to maximise expected profit is **200 units**

Produce a payoff table:

| Demand | Probability | | Supply | |
|---|---|---|---|---|
| | | 100 | 200 | 300 |
| 100 units | 0.25 | $400 | $0 (W1) | ($400) (W2) |
| 200 units | 0.40 | $400 | $800 | $400 (W3) |
| 300 units | 0.35 | $400 | $800 | $1,200 |

**Workings**

| (W1) | $100 \times \$8 - 200 \times \$4$ | = | $0 |
|---|---|---|---|
| (W2) | $100 \times \$8 - 300 \times \$4$ | = | ($400) |
| (W3) | $200 \times \$8 - 300 \times \$4$ | = | $400 |

Expected profits:

| If supply 100 units, EVs | = | | $400 |
|---|---|---|---|
| If supply 200 units, EV = $0 × 0.25 + $800 × 0.4 + $800 × 0.35 | | = | $600 |
| If supply 300 units, EV = ($400) × 0.25 + $400 × 0.4 + $1,200 × 0.35 | | = | $480 |

∴ Profit is maximised by supplying 200 units.

**195** The probability that the weekly contribution will exceed $20,000 is **45%**

To generate a contribution greater than $20,000 it is necessary to earn a unit contribution greater than $20. Consider each of the feasible combinations:

| Selling price | Variable cost | Contribution | Probability |
|---|---|---|---|
| $ | $ | $ | |
| 50 | 20 | 30 | 0.45 × 0.55 = 0.2475 |
| 60 | 20 | 40 | 0.25 × 0.55 = 0.1375 |
| 60 | 30 | 30 | 0.25 × 0.25 = 0.0625 |
| | | **Answer =** | **0.4475** |

Answer = 44.75% = 45% to nearest full %

**196  B**

| Project | EV | Workings |
|---|---|---|
| | $000 | |
| L | 500 | (500 × 0.2) + (470 × 0.5) + (550 × 0.3) |
| M | 526 | (400 × 0.2) + (550 × 0.5) + (570 × 0.3) |
| N | 432.5 | (450 × 0.2) + (400 × 0.5) + (475 × 0.3) |
| O | 398 | etc. |
| P | 497.5 | |

∴ Project M will maximise expected cash.

## 197  D

If market condition is forecast as Poor, then Project P should be chosen as this project yields the highest cash flow under a poor market.

However, if the market condition is forecast as Good or Excellent, then Project M should be chosen as M will yield the highest cash.

In summary:

| Market condition | Selected project | Cash (x) $000 | Probability (p) | px |
|---|---|---|---|---|
| Poor | P | 600 | 0.20 | 120 |
| Good | M | 550 | 0.50 | 275 |
| Excellent | M | 570 | 0.30 | 171 |
| | | | 1.00 | 566 |

| | |
|---|---|
| Expected return with perfect information | $566,000 |
| Expected return without (answer to 1.2) | $526,000 |
| ∴ Value of information | $40,000 |

## 198  Assuming the baker adopts the minimax regret decision rule, the number of batches of bread that he should bake each day is 12 batches

| Contribution table | | Daily demand | | |
|---|---|---|---|---|
| | | 10 | 11 | 12 |
| | 10 (W1) | 500 | 500 | 500 |
| Batches baked | 11 (W2) | 480 | 550 | 550 |
| | 12 (W3) | 460 | 530 | 600 |

**Workings**

(W1)  If 10 batches are baked they will all be sold earning a contribution of $500

(W2)  If 11 batches are baked and 10 are sold this earns a contribution of $10 \times 50 - 20 = 480$

(W3)  If 12 batches are baked and 10 are sold contribution = $10 \times 50 - 40 = 460$

A regret table can now be produced which shows the shortfall from the maximum contribution that could be earned at each demand level. So, if demand is 12 batches, the maximum contribution is $600. If only 10 batches are baked, the contribution earned is $500, a regret of $100.

| Regret table | | Daily demand | | | |
|---|---|---|---|---|---|
| | | 10 | 11 | 12 | Max. Regret |
| | 10 | 0 | 50 | 100 | 100 |
| Batches baked | 11 | 20 | 0 | 50 | 50 |
| | 12 | 40 | 20 | 0 | 40 |

So to minimise the maximum regret the baker should bake 12 batches.

**199**

| Decision criteria | Attitude to risk |
|---|---|
| Expected values | Risk neutral |
| Maximax | Risk seeker |
| Maximin | Risk averse |
| Minimax regret | Risk averse |

**200  A**

The expected value is

= -2m + [(0.8 x 9.2m) + (0.2 x -1m)] = $5.16m

**201  B**

Minimax regret table:

| Demand | Order level | | | |
|---|---|---|---|---|
| | 20 bunches | 30 bunches | 40 bunches | 50 bunches |
| 20 bunches | $0 | $40 ** | $80 | $120 |
| 30 bunches | $30 | $0 | $40 | $80 |
| 40 bunches | $60 | $30 | $0 | $40 |
| 50 bunches | $90 | $60 | $30 | $0 |

** *Working:*

*If demand is 20 bunches, the optimum order level would have been 20 bunches. In this situation a profit of $60 would have been made (as per payoff table). This is the maximum profit available for a demand of 20.*

*If Chris had ordered 30 bunches instead of 20 then he would have ordered too many and would have made a profit of just $20, therefore the value of the regret is the difference between the optimum profit and the actual profit. In this case the regret would be $60 – $20 = $40.*

The maximum regret for 20 bunches is $90

The maximum regret for 30 bunches is $60

The maximum regret for 40 bunches is $80

The maximum regret for 50 bunches is $120

If the company wishes to minimise the maximum regret 30 bunches should be ordered.

**202  A**

The value of perfect information=

Expected profit with the information – expected profit without the information.

In this scenario the value of the perfect information is $15,000.

The expected profit without the information is $142,000.

Therefor the expected profit with the information is $142,000 + $15,000 = $157,000

**203** **The probability that lowering the selling price to $45 per unit would increase profit is 82%**

*Joint Contribution*
*probability  $000*

|  |  |
|---|---|
| 0.18 | 2,500 (W1) |
| 0.27 | 2,700 (W2) |
| 0.22 | 3,000 (W3) |
| 0.33 | 3,240 (W4) |
| 1.00 | |

Existing contribution =   ($50 – $21) × 90,000 units = 2,610 ($000)

Contribution is greater than this in (W2), (W3) and (W4) above.

∴ The probability of the profit being higher is = 0.27 + 0.22 + 0.33 =  0.82

**Workings**

| | |
|---|---|
| (W1) | ($45 – $20) × 100,000 units |
| (W2) | ($45 – $18) × 100,000 units |
| (W3) | ($45 – $20) × 120,000 units |
| (W4) | ($45 – $18) × 120,000 units |

**204** **The expected value of the company profit if the selling price is reduced to $45 per unit is $1,708,200**

Expected demand:

(100,000 × 0.45) + (120,000 × 0.55)     111,000 units

Expected variable cost:

($20 × 0.40) + ($18 × 0.60)          $18.80

Contribution per unit:

$45 – $18.80                 $26.20


Expected contribution:

111,000 × $26.20          $2,908,200

Less fixed costs           ($1,200,000)


Expected profit             $1,708,200

**205** **The probability that the variance is less than $45,000 is 0.13%**

The mean is $60,000. $45,000 is $15,000 away from the mean.

This represents $15,000/$5,000 = 3.00 standard deviations. This is the z score.

From tables, on the left hand column, look up the z score to one decimal place, i.e. 3.0. Look along this row until it meets the column with the 2nd decimal place (0.00). The table gives us 0.4987.

This means that when looking at the 50% of variances that are below the mean 49.87% of them are within 3 standard deviations. Therefore, the probability that the variance will be below $45,000 is the remaining 0.13%

**206** **D**

| Expected selling price | | Expected cost | |
|---|---|---|---|
| | $ | | $ |
| $20 × 0.25 | 5 | $8 × 0.2 | 1.6 |
| $25 × 0.4 | 10 | $10 × 0.5 | 5 |
| 330 × 0.35 | 10.5 | $12 × 0.3 | 3.6 |
| | 25.5 | | 10.2 |

Expected unit contribution = $25.50 – $10.20 = $15.30 × 1,000 = $15,300

**207** **C**

Monthly contribution will exceed $13,500 if unit contribution exceeds $13.50. This will be the case for the following combinations:

| Sales price | Variable cost | Probability | Joint probability |
|---|---|---|---|
| $25 | $8 | 0.4 × 0.2 | 0.08 |
| $25 | $10 | 0.4 × 0.5 | 0.20 |
| $30 | ($8) | | |
| $30 | ($10) | 0.35 × 1 | 0.35 |
| $30 | ($12) | | |
| Total | | | 0.63 |

**208** **B**

The minimum outcome for a fee of $600 is $360k

The minimum outcome for a fee of $800 is $400k

The minimum outcome for a fee of $900 is $360k

The minimum outcome for a fee of $1,000 is $320k

Therefore if the committee wants to maximise the minimum cash inflow it will set a fee of $800.

## 209   A

A regret matrix is shown below:

| Membership fee | Membership level | | |
|---|---|---|---|
| | Low $000 | Average $000 | High $000 |
| $600 | 40 | 0 | 0 |
| $800 | 0 | 40 | 60 |
| $900 | 40 | 75 | 45 |
| $1,000 | 80 | 100 | 120 |

Maximum regret if set fee of $600 is $40k

Maximum regret if set fee of $800 is $60k

Maximum regret if set fee of $900 is $75k

Maximum regret if set fee of $1,000 is $120k

To minimise the maximum regret a fee of $600 should be set.

## 210   The number of cakes Sarah should bake if she applies the maximax decision criterion is 30.

If Sarah applied the maximax decision criterion she would bake 30 cakes each day as the maximum contribution of $21 is to be gained at this level.

## 211   The number of cakes Sarah should bake if she applies the maximin decision criterion is 20.

| | Number of cakes baked | | |
|---|---|---|---|
| | 20 | 25 | 30 |
| Worst contribution | $14 | $11.5 | $9 |

If Sarah baked 20 cakes the worst contribution would be $14, this is the best "worst contribution"

If Sarah applied the maximax decision criterion she would bake 30 cakes each day as the maximum contribution of $21 is to be gained at this level.

## 212   A

Perfect information is always 100% accurate. By comparison imperfect information is usually correct but can be incorrect.

## 213   B

The maximum regret for product W is $43,000

The maximum regret for product X is $17,000

The maximum regret for product Y is $73,000

The maximum regret for product Z is $38,000

**214  B**

Point G represents a decision point. If the decision is taken to licence then there is a value of $6m.

The other decision is to further invest – which appears to have a cost of $4m. But this then opens up the chance point where there is a 70% chance of making $22m and a 30% chance of making $9m. So this decision to further invest would have an expected value of:

= -4m + [(0.7 x 22) + (0.3 x 9)] = $14.1m

Therefore, the decision to further invest is worth more than the licencing option. The company would choose to invest and would make $14.1m.

**215  The maximum amount that should be paid for the information from the market research company is $7,500.**

The value of perfect information is calculated as:

Expected value with perfect information – Expected value without perfect information.

*Expected value without perfect information:*

The expected value without perfect information is $880,000.

*Expected value with perfect information:*

| Demand | Sales price | Profit (x) | Prob (p) | px |
|--------|-------------|------------|----------|-----|
| High | $105 | $1,725,000 | 30% | $517,500 |
| Medium | $100 | $700,000 | 50% | $350,000 |
| Low | $100 | $100,000 | 20% | $20,000 |
| | | | EV | **$887,500** |

The value of perfect information is $887,500 – $880,000 = $7,500

**216  C**

The information provided by the meteorologist is called imperfect information. The value of imperfect information is calculated in the same way as the value of perfect information:

Expected profit with the information – expected profit without the information.

In this scenario we already know the value of the information: Soggy is prepared to pay $30,000 for the information.

We have also been told that the expected profit with the information is $1,250,000.

We therefore have to calculate the expected profit without the information:

= $1,250,000 – $30,000 = $1,220,000

**217** **The maximum amount that should be paid for the information from the market research company is $11,440.**

The value of perfect information is calculated as:

Expected value with perfect information – Expected value without perfect information.

*Expected value without perfect information:*

The expected value without perfect information is $719,700.

*Expected value with perfect information:*

| Demand | Shop size | Profit (x) | Prob (p) | px |
|--------|-----------|------------|----------|-----|
| Strong | LARGE | 1,413,200 | 0.2 | 282,640 |
| Good | LARGE | 865,700 | 0.4 | 346,280 |
| Weak | MEDIUM | 255,550 | 0.4 | 102,220 |
| | | | Expected value | 731,140 |

The value of perfect information is $731,140 – $719,700 = $11,440

**218** **The expected value at point A on the decision trees (to the nearest $0.1m) is $22m**

Point A represents a decision point. If the decision is taken to outsource then there is a value of $22m.

The other decision is to further invest – which appears to have a cost of $20m. But this then opens up the chance point where there is a 60% chance of making $60m and a 40% chance of making $12m. So this decision to further invest would have an expected value of:

= -20m + [(0.6 x 60) + (0.4 x 12)] = $20.8m

Therefore, the decision to further invest is worth less than the outsourcing option. The company would choose to outsource and would make $22m.

**219** **Using expected values, the financial benefit from engaging MS for the concert is $915**

The expected audience size = (0.5 x 300) + (0.3 x 400) + (0.2 x 500) = 370

The expected contribution = 370 x [(0.7 x 25) + (0.3 x 40)] = $10,915

The financial benefit from engaging MS is $10,915 – $10,000 = $915

Therefore it is worthwhile engaging MS for the concert.

**220** **Which of the following are disadvantages of using an expected value technique?**

| | Disadvantage of EVs? |
|---|---|
| Expected values only provides the most likely result | |
| It ignores attitudes to risk | ✓ |
| Only two possible outcomes can be considered | |
| Probabilities are subjective | ✓ |
| The answer provided may not exist | ✓ |

ing investigations into her involvement with groups of insurgents and the assets of her estate were being impounded. Watching footage of the cabinet arriving at Parliament House, Kouranis stepping out of a burgundy Aston Martin DB7. And Shake knows that Kouranis has found himself a highly desirable week-end residence on St George, a mansion with marble floors, travertine tables and an infinity pool, looking out over Gilbey beach. And maybe, as Kouranis sits out by the pool, drinking his champagne, he can look down at his boat bobbing in the water. Perhaps it will be a Bertram 31, with a sky-blue canopy, the paint-work dulled where the name *Ribailagua* has been erased? Perhaps it has a new Pompanette fighting chair fixed on the deck? Shake sat in the bungalow and watched the coverage of the coup begin-ning to slip as Mugabe roared and the women ran again through sandstorms in Darfur.

Shake often sits on the porch with his beer and thinks about Susannah, tries to imagine what happened to her because he knows her magenta heart would never have stopped beating unless forced to. She had been killed because she was too rich to ignore; she was too bold, too angry, too unloved for Kouranis to ignore. Susannah loved her nation, she may have reviled each and every person in it, may have cussed and shouted but she loved her nation and she could stand up to Kouranis the Greek. Nothing but a fucking Phoenician trader. Susannah would have shouted to the last, would have died for the land, for the pickneys who stood at standpipes in the street to wash, died for the ragged nowherians.

Book close.

But book isn't close because Shake can't forget St George. He misses it every moment of every day. As he drinks his beer on the porch, Shake listens for the tree frogs and the bleat of a goat, waits for the booming bass which shudders the floor blasting from a passing car but there is silence. He looks in the trees for fireflies, checks the walls for scurrying geckos but there are none. He misses the sight of black hands swirling scythes, zagai, and grasses flying. The taste of coconut water, cut on the back of a truck, the sight of palm trees black against a palely darkening sky, the smell of mosquito coils, the red and gold, ice-beaded label of an S&G bottle. He misses the brown puppies, dus'bin terriers, who eat from the garbage cages, misses the walnut taste of avocados the size of footballs, the sweetness of dolphin meat, the crashing thud of a coconut falling. Misses driving barefoot, a beastly cold beer in his hand. He misses his hammock, he misses Saltbag and his beachside conversations with the venerable Mister Jeremiah. He misses hearing news about Miss Avarice and her feets, about her heart. Misses not understanding Miss Lizbeth. He misses Rajiv, who is safe, now, in Frankfurt and doing what he does best — making money. Shake misses Avril, thinks about her petite black hands turning kingfish in the pan.

Shake showers and changes into a hot shirt and chinos, heads for the bar, driving through Sag Harbor, down to the water and he looks at the houses lining the street, thinks of his concrete house which was never finished. Dragon never even raised the red flag, never tied the roofbeams. Shake's one stab at building a home and it failed. His one stab at being someone, being some-one in the right place and still he has to be bailed out, as he has been all his life. By his girlfriends at university, by Emma, by Rajiv, by Avril and Susannah. And now by Mr Westmore, whose income does indeed exceed his outgoings, even though he owns a house in Greenwich, a house on the island, a yacht and a sixty-foot powerboat, even though he owns the bar where Shake is parking a car owned by Mr Westmore, his income exceeds his outgoings. Shake wonders, as he pushes open the door, to be greeted by the hubbub of mild, milky drinkers, if Mr Westmore owns Shake.

The bar is highly polished oak, red stools fixed in front, a long, etched mirror running the length of the wall behind. Mr Westmore, once he had put Shake back together again, appointed him manager, said the bar needed shaking up. Laughed. So Shake shook. The bar is not el Floridita, is not el Bodeguita del Medio, but it is now called Ribailagua's and it's jumping every night as the cocktails flow. Thursday night is rum night, when every drink is based on white or dark rum and Shake knocks up not only Mai Tai and Planters' Punch but also Reef Juice, Painkiller, Goombay Smash and Bees Knees Martini 1 but he won't make a Caribbean Breeze, no matter how nicely the customer asks. He makes daiquiris and Oh Gosh!, Palermo and Honeysuckle'tini but he refuses to make mojitos. For his cocktails he buys only branded juices and liquor – Schweppes and Ocean Spray, fresh squeezed juices, Rose's lime cordial. Behind the bar, amongst the jars of freshly limes, the sprigs of mint, the sugar cubes and Angostura bitters, the Waring blenders gleam. Shake buys Bombay Sapphire gin, Passoã, Sauza Hornitos tequila. But he will not buy Huggins' single mark because Susannah is dead and he can't buy Havana Club Tres Años because it comes from an island where the Americans like to keep their prisoners but don't like to drink the rum.

This Thursday night the bar is heaving and Shake has his back turned to the bar, searching in an icebox for fresh raspberries, when he hears the woman call for a mojito. He turns round and sees a cowgirl standing by the bar, tapping it impatiently. She looks as if she's run away from the circus, escaped from the rodeo. Shake never makes a mojito but he offers her a Papa Dobles Special and she accepts. He pours a double measure of Myers, a single of grapefruit juice, a third ounce of maraschino liqueur and crushed ice into a shaker. Then he drops a lime into boiling water and waits the longest half minute of his life, watching his fingers pulse, before twitching the fruit from the bowl and rolling it beneath his palm, pressing it down on the marble board. Selecting a knife, the sharpest, cruellest knife, he slices the fruit, squeezes half the juice into the shaker and then agitates the shaker in a short, violent burst. He strains the drink into a double martini glass, pouring it over a sparkling mound of crushed ice and hands it to the cowgirl. She takes the glass, sips, smells the scent of lime and drinks the daiquiri down in one.

'That's damn good,' she says, tipping her hat.

'On the house,' says Shake. 'On the house.'